This book is a joyous, challen̦   ..umen
everywhere. And having read iɩ   ., Why did God
give so many gifts to Heather?   ..ɔus said, Freely you have
received, freely give. (Matthew 10:8) Could it be because she
was so yielded to God and so trusted Him for His faithful
provision that she was so free to give what He had given her?
And as she kept on giving He just kept on giving her more? May
God, through this book touch you, His beloved, that through
faith, commitment and obedience you too will be blessed with
His abundant giftings.

Alan Penberthy

Heather Double's transfer to Heaven has left a large gap in
many of our lives, but equally her life furnished us with so many
precious memories. What a treasury has been compiled as a wide
variety of people touched by Heather have shared their thoughts
and memories. Heather lives on in our hearts, and the example
she set in life, continues to be reflected in many who were
influenced by her. The manner in which she faced the fleeting
experience of death will be a comfort to all who recognise their
true hope in Christ. This book is timely, uplifting and honours
a true woman of God

Dr. Tony Stone

Heather lived an abundant life. She learned how to receive from
an abundant God, and like Him, learned how to give herself and
her knowledge away. This book will challenge you to live like she
lived and to follow her example!

Joyce and Charles Sibthorpe

Course You Can!

Inspiration and encouragement from
the life story of

Heather Double

as told by her husband

DON DOUBLE
with Gwen Macmillan

Course You Can!
© 2008 Don Double
All rights reserved
Published by Summit Publishing Ltd, Milton Keynes.
www.summitpublishing.co.uk

ISBN 978-1-901074-18-5

Unless otherwise noted, Scripture quotations are taken from the *New International Version* NIV © 1973, 1978, 1984 by the International Bible Society. Used by permission.

Scripture marked TLB is taken from *The Living Bible*, copyright © 1971. Used by permission of Tyndale House Publishers, Inc., Wheaton, Illinois 60189.

Scripture marked AMP is taken from the *Amplified Bible* Copyright © 1954, 1958, 1962, 1964, 1965, 1987 by The Lockman Foundation.

Scripture marked MSG is taken from *The Message*. Copyright © 1993, 1994, 1995, 1996, 2000, 2001, 2002. Used by permission of NavPress Publishing Group.

Printed in the United Kingdom by Creative Print and Design Wales.

1 2 3 4 5 6 7 8 9 10 / 12 11 10 09 08

Dedication

*I dedicate this book to all those who, like Heather,
are seeking to know and fulfil their calling in God,
whatever the cost.*

Hymn to a Good Wife

A good woman is hard to find,
and worth far more than diamonds.
Her husband trusts her without reserve,
and never has reason to regret it.
Never spiteful, she treats him generously
all her life long.

When she speaks she has something worthwhile to say,
and she always says it kindly.

"Many women have done wonderful things,
but you've outclassed them all!"
Charm can mislead and beauty soon fades.
The woman to be admired and praised
is the woman who lives in the Fear-of-God.

From Proverbs 31 MSG

Contents

Acknowledgements

Heather and I have written many books over the years, as well as those we have co-authored together, but this one is very different in that it is the life story of the one I shared my life with for over 43 years and who I miss greatly.

First of all I want to acknowledge God's wonderful gift to me in Heather and to thank Him for everything that He allowed us to share together.

I want to thank Him too for the special family He entrusted to our care and upbringing, all of whom have helped to make us and shape us along the way.

Together Heather and I were a great team, but as God expanded our ministry we couldn't have done what we did without a bigger team. Therefore, I want to thank God for all those who have served on the GNC team with us over the years, and to the many from this nation and overseas who have been so faithful to us in prayer, support and friendship.

Heather was one who valued people and who God had made them to be, so I want to pay my own tribute to all those who have enriched Heather's life as she sought to share her life with you.

In order for this book to become a reality, I am aware that many of you have made contributions which have helped to weave together a beautiful tapestry in Heather's memory, and as a testimony to the grace of God.

Lastly, I want to thank David Clark for his careful proof-reading of the text and Noël Halsey and Linda Finley-Day of *Summit Publishing* for the publication of this book in record time!

I appreciate you all.

God bless you.

Don Double

Introduction

When Heather dreamed of writing her next book it was to be that of her own autobiography, bearing the title *My Story*, which she began to write in 2007. In fact she even took her computer into the Hospice with her so she could continue with her writing. However, after being told she only had weeks to live, on the 10th February she wrote this request in her personal journal: "I have been trying to write *My Story* and I hope someone will be able to take it on and finish it for me, as I feel this is one of the things God has asked me to do." This book is the result.

Thinking that there would be lots of "someone's" who would offer to help fulfil Heather's dream in some way, Gwen Macmillan, who knew Heather well, offered to complete the book for me. As I often say "he or she who gets the vision gets the job" and she accepted this as a real privilege, desiring to honour Heather as a woman of God whom she loved and greatly appreciated as a friend. I deeply appreciate and thank Gwen for accepting this responsibility and for everything she has done to help make one of Heather's last requests a reality.

For many years Gwen has been involved with us both through evangelism and camps. In fact, it was Gwen, and her late husband Peter Cobb, from Bury St. Edmunds, Suffolk, who co-ordinated all our Chadacre Family Camps, and who later served on the GNC Unit team at many of our Malvern Camps. Now re-married and living in Oxford, where they pastor a Church, both Terry and Gwen Macmillan maintain their prayer and friendship links with us and serve at our annual Family Camps.

The title of this book, *Course You Can!* was born out of the fact that it was a phrase often used by Heather as both a challenge and encouraging response to those who hesitated in taking new steps of faith or obedience. It was particularly highlighted in a tribute brought at Heather's 'Thanksgiving Service' at our Taunton Family Camp in 2007 by a friend, Anne Trahearn. Later in the week, in addressing an evening gathering as guest speaker at the same Camp, Dan Sneed (who wrote the foreword to this book) also referred to Heather's words as being a fitting book title!

Heather's life was never dull and I can never remember her ever being bored. She was always actively doing something! In fact, she became the most creative person I have ever known, writing books, newsletters, dressmaking, creative cooking, drawing, painting, all forms of needlework and crafts, to name but a few!

Woven throughout Heather's life story are particular references to Scripture, life-application teaching and experiences recorded in her own journals which illustrate something of her own personal walk with the Lord. As you read through this book, I am sure you will appreciate that all writers have their own style, and although I endorse everything that Gwen has written with me, and for me, it is in her style, which is different from some of my earlier books. But it fully reflects my heart and the truth of all that Heather and I shared together in life and ministry and I pray that its freshness will bless, encourage and challenge you in your own faith and obedience to God.

I hope that we, together with so many of our family, friends and colleagues who have kindly contributed, have captured something of Heather's multi-faceted life through the pages of *Course You Can!*

One thing is certain, Heather would want all the Praise and Glory to go to her personal Lord, Saviour and Friend, **the Lord Jesus Christ**, for all that HE did in and through her life.

Don Double

Foreword

As long as I live I'll never forget the words *Course You Can!* They've marked my life! When Heather Double would say them they always sounded more like one long Cornish word "courseyoucan", but everyone knew what she meant. Whatever challenges you faced, whatever the difficulty before you, even when it seemed impossible, with God *of course you can*, face it, do it and even triumph over it! Heather was a very practical woman filled with faith. Or I could say she was a woman of faith who knew how to make it work practically in everyday life.

I've known Don and Heather for almost four decades. We first met in the pouring rain in northern England not far from the Scottish border. It was my first British summer camp experience at a place called Blaithwaite. I'm not sure why they called it a summer camp, it didn't seem like summer at all to me. It was cold, it rained all week and the mud was half way to our knees. People sat wrapped in blankets, drinking hot tea while rain water streamed down the aisles of the tent where we were meeting. That was the setting for my first encounter with this amazing woman, who touched so many lives in so many places. Since that time, we've been together in numerous summer camps, retreat centres and conferences. I've stayed in their home in

Cornwall and they've been in our's in California. I've seen them in good times and watched them in times of incredible pressure and difficulty. They are two very ordinary people who have lived extraordinary lives.

There are so many things I could say about the impact of Heather's life. She was an extremely gifted teacher who could make deep spiritual truths very practical and understandable to everyone who heard her. She loved people and valued them for who they were and what she believed God could do with their lives. Heather was a woman of great faith who simply loved Jesus and deeply believed that He loved her and the people around her. When you were discouraged or stressed and felt like giving up, saying things like "I can't do this" — "it's too hard" — "I don't have what it takes" — she would simply speak the words that have come to mark her life; words that I'm sure she had spoken to herself over and over again "Of course you can" — with God's help you **can** do it! And she believed it!

As you read this book and celebrate Heather's life with us, remember she was an ordinary woman touched by the hand of God. She was willing to face life's challenges, to obey God's voice and to take the risks, always believing, with God's help, "of course you can!" or as Heather would say it "courseyoucan".

Dan Sneed

1

My Story

*As written by Heather herself in the final
months of her life's journey*

Most books appear to have a foreword, introduction or preface before you get into the real material. As an avid reader, I often find myself missing these because so many of them ramble on and in some cases are irrelevant and add nothing to the rest of the book. So, I have avoided such a beginning— wanting to get right on with the subject!

To really tell my story (because of the person I am), there will be times when I intersperse with a little teaching, or things that I feel God has spoken to me and taught me over the years. I would also like to pay tribute to all those who, have contributed to who I am.

From the time my mother became a 'born again' Christian, there have been those who have prayed for me. In particular I think of four spinsters who were her close friends and prayed for us as a family. Who I am today is because such people have taken the time to pray, support, be friends—and taken an interest. I know there are hundreds around the world that pray for Don and I, and each one of them are of value to us and have added to who we are. Many look at what we have accomplished over time and are appreciative of what we have done, but I believe each one of those who have prayed, supported and been involved in the ministry will be part of the reward because we could not have done it without you all.

My Story, as I call it, is only a small part of a much bigger picture.

The Word of God says that *He will fulfil His purpose for us* (Psalm 57:2) and I am a firm believer in the purposes of God. I am sure that God is preparing His people upon earth for the real purposes of Heaven. No matter what we accomplish on this earth, Heaven is the goal—and what we are there is reality.

Matthew 6, verse 19 tells us not to store up treasures here on earth where they can be eaten by moths and get rusty, and where thieves break in and steal. But to *"Store up for yourselves treasures in heaven, where moth and rust do not destroy, and where thieves do not break in and steal. For where your treasure is, there your heart will be also."* (Matthew 6:20-21)

No matter what we accomplish here on this earth, what really matters are the treasures that are stored up for us in Heaven. Many people on this earth put their trust in money, possessions and the like, but those who are God's children have an inheritance in Heaven which far exceeds anything we could amass on this earth.

Those who have been 'behind the scenes' praying, interceding and supporting in every way (including financially)—becoming real friends and partners—are all 'storing up treasures in Heaven'!

To understand the shaping of the person I am, we have to begin before my birthday on the 20th May 1944. My parents, John and Rhoda Martin, were married in July 1939, just two months before World War II began. They both came from families who were regular Church members. My mother and father were first cousins—my father's mother and my mother's father being brother and sister. This meant that we did not have a vast number of uncles, cousins and family relations (although my grandfather and grandmother had 12 brothers and sisters).

My father was raised in North Devon, living in Torrington, going to school in Barnstaple, and being an active member of the Congregational Church. His parents ran a thriving hotel and inn. His father was a qualified chef. Starting his career in the Royal Navy, he rose to become an Officer in the Royal Navy. My mother was brought up in Laira, a suburb of Plymouth, where her father worked as a wagon repairer for the Railways, and their whole family was involved in the Methodist Church. When they were married my father was given a commission in Cyprus, but—because of the war—this never materialized.

When my father left to go to war, my parents covenanted together that wherever they were in the world at 9 p.m. they would read their Bibles and pray, even though at this stage of their lives they had no real 'born again' experience. It would be a number of years after the war that they would come to know Jesus as their personal Saviour and Lord.

During the war my father was stationed on various naval vessels, two of which were sunk—one on the Mediterranean Sea (H.M.S. Hermione)—when it was eighteen hours before he was picked out of the sea, after seeing his boyhood friend give up and 'go under'. The other H.M.S. Curlew (one of the first naval vessels to have radar), was sunk above the Arctic Circle at a place called Narvik.

While awaiting a boat to take them back to the UK, he and his friend attended morning prayers in the local Monastery where nun's were looking after refugee children from Norwegian cities. During one of the morning sessions of prayer three 'peeps' on the harbour hooter summoned all naval personnel to get to the harbour as there would be transport for them back to the UK. My father and his friend would not disturb the morning Mass, so remained. This ship was actually sunk, and I am led to believe there were no survivors. It was another three weeks before there was another vessel to bring my father back to the UK.

After this time he was placed in North Africa with the British Army, during the famous El Alamein battle, and spent many weeks in the desert repairing guns and driving tanks.

During the first 12 years of their married life my parents were together for just six weeks!

My brother was born in March 1941, after one of his visits home, and—as I have already said—I was born in May 1944, after another one of his visits home! Many times my mother told me how she dedicated me to God before I was born. This I believe was the foundation of all that has happened in my life. Obviously this all contributed to my upbringing and how we were taught about the war, and other cultural things.

Being devout 'Church goers', my parents and grandparents (on both sides) had a basis of God in their lives. This meant that I also had grounded into me a belief that God existed and was relevant to us.

It is one of my firm beliefs that, as parents, how we train our children and what we instil in them will determine who they are, and what they become. As Christians, the model of our own walk with God will speak to them. When my children were small I used to pray (audibly) and read my Bible as I sat with them as they played. I did not hide my faith and trust in God. I involved them in praying for our provision. With Don so often away on the mission field and travelling, I had set a goal in my own faith that every time he came home from a trip on the mission field or overseas, there would be no bills that had to be paid. I know if you could ask him today, he would tell you that was just what happened. When we were in need of something—clothes for school, food for the table, or petrol for the car—we would pray together and see God's provision. They were involved with us, our ministry and our faith. I believed that the grace of God was upon them for the calling that He had put upon their parents just as much as it was upon us. Children learn more by watching and seeing than by words, and this is especially true with our faith and walk with God. How they see us relate to our Heavenly Father will influence them.

My father did not finish his naval career until 1948 as he was in the Japanese war. On his return home he was two and a half years in hospital for medical treatment. Very early on in the war he had broken his wrist and had lived with it because there was never time for him to go to hospital and have it repaired. Twice he was put in hospital to attempt repair. Once was in Beirut, Lebanon, but it was deemed too risky in the heat to undergo surgery. Another time he was here in the UK, but was recalled to refit another ship before it could begin. He was 'disabled' out of the Navy and told he would need to lead a 'quiet' life because of the injuries received during the war.

It was not until 1951 that I really knew that I had a father. In those days it was common for families to live in close proximity. The village I was brought up in—St. Blazey Gate, near St. Austell, Cornwall—was one such community. Both sets of grandparents had returned to their 'roots' during the war years. Their fathers were the local game keeper and head gardener for the Carlyon Estate. (Anyone familiar with the St. Austell area will know of the connection, and also know that estate known as Tregrehan House). A terrace, known as Edgcumbe Terrace, was the location of our family. In No.19 lived my mother's parents. We lived in No.21. My father's parents lived in No.22! We all attended the local Methodist Church, where my mother's parents had been the first ones on the register to be married when the Church received its licence.

This Church was known as 'Leek Seed'. The name came from the story that a local man who was a keen gardener and also the caretaker for the land where the Church was being erected. One night his room was broken into and the burglars demanded the money that had been collected to build the Church. By his bed was a sack of leek seed, which evidently looks like dynamite, and he threatened to blow them all up by igniting this 'dynamite' if they did not leave! They left immediately — and so the Church was named 'Leek Seed'.

My early years were centred on life in the village and the Church. When I was nine, my mother had a real experience with God. Her life changed — and so did mine — and the rest of the family. It would be a number of years before my father surrendered his life to Christ, but in the meantime my mother took me to many different meetings, a few of which stand out in my memory. At one in the Guild Hall at Devonport, Plymouth, I watched a man with a 'hunchback' walk off the platform after being prayed for — perfectly upright with a 'sack' in the back of his jacket where his 'hunchback' had been! In the same meeting I witnessed a deaf and dumb brother and sister (twins) hear each other speak for the first time in their lives! I began to realize that God was real and alive.

Another meeting was in Mevagissey, during which the Pastor (Henry Shave), when praying for me, gave a word that I would receive a 'double portion' of the Spirit of God. I often say that God has a sense of humour as just ten years later I would change my name to 'Double'!

There were other incidents that remain in my memory that have had great influences in my life. My mother at this time had become friendly with the local 'Christian' community and was invited to a morning meeting in a lady's home. She went along with her friend, but became very suspicious when they entered the room where the curtains were drawn, with very low lighting. The meeting opened with Bible reading and prayer and my mother began to pray and ask that the 'Blood of Jesus' would cover and protect them. Immediately following this prayer the lady leading the meeting said, "I cannot contact my spirit today. All I can see is a wall of blood." My mother and her friend immediately departed, and later learnt that this lady was a spiritualist! My, how that story has lived with me and taught me to have faith in the Blood of Jesus.

Right from my earliest memory, my parents 'gave' themselves to others. A very vivid memory is of a Friday night, which was 'bath night'! As soon as our meal was over my father and I would visit some of the elderly widows in the village, taking them gifts—mostly made up of vegetables and flowers which my parents grew—then it was home for bath and bed.

Then there was the couple who had one son. The mother became seriously ill mentally, so my parents took on care for their son while the father was at work during the day. Terry became like a brother to me. Then one of my cousins became part of our family because of problems within their family. So my early years taught me to share; not just what you had, but 'yourself', with those in need.

One day my brother came home with a bad injury to his nose. When Mum enquired what had happened, he said it was OK—he just fell on some barbed wire! This was not surprising when you consider in those days, as children brought up in the 'country', we had free range of various woodlands, farmland, cliffs and other free roaming places. After a few days when the injury looked no better, but rather worse, the truth came out. My brother had been shot with an air rifle! An X-ray showed very clearly the pellet embedded in his nose. Surgery was planned, but Mum prayed before he went for surgery. She requested another X-ray—which was refused! The surgeon promised my brother that he would give him the pellet after the operation. My brother never received the pellet because the surgeon could not find it!

Once again God was proving Himself to be a God of miracles.

These were the things that shaped my early life, and were the foundation of my own personal walk with God. Until this time I knew about God—had been taught very firmly that God was a real live person who existed—but there was nothing personal in my own life. Yes, I read my Bible as any young child brought up in this environment would do. I went to Church and was 'involved' but it was still not personal. God only has children. He does not have grand-children, nor even great grand-children!

Over the years I have been fascinated by the life of Abraham. Throughout the Bible our God is called 'the God of Abraham, Isaac and Jacob'. Abraham appears to be one of the main foundational personalities and patriarchs. I have read and studied his life and God has often spoken to me from his story. One of the things that fascinated me was the number of altars he built. There were only four, but one was visited twice. As I looked at these altars I realized that they are all relevant to our lives. As I relate 'My Story' I am going to intersperse it with these altars because they have become relevant to me.

The first time I can actually remember God answering a prayer for me personally was my 11 Plus. For those not familiar with it, back then every child had to take an examination at the age of 11 to see which senior school they were to attend. If you passed, you went to the local Grammar School. If you failed, you went to the Secondary Modern School. I had been told by my Head Master that there was no way I would pass this 11 Plus exam. All my friends would, but I would not! This sent me to prayer. I can remember getting on my knees by my bed before I went to sleep asking God to help me pass the

11 Plus. When the day came for the results to be announced my name was the first on the list of those who had passed! Not that I believe that meant anything, but it did to me. God had answered MY prayer. This meant that He really was real and active for ME.This began my search for God. From that day on something happened in my life. This to me is my first altar of Abraham, when God revealed Himself to me for the first time on a personal basis. A prayer I prayed and God had answered.

Genesis 12, verse 7 records God speaking to Abraham. This is the first time we hear that Abraham heard God. His response was immediate obedience. In verse 4 we read *so Abraham departed as the Lord had instructed him.* There should be a response when we hear God. This altar I call an 'altar of acceptance'. Acceptance of God that He is; that He exists, and that He is interested in us as an individual. For many this will be a time of salvation and acceptance of Jesus as their Lord and Saviour. For others, like me, it will be a place where we acknowledge that God is interested in ME. We have been raised in a 'Christian' atmosphere and many things have still to be worked out in our own walk with God.

I believe these places are actually real places that we can remember where, when and what. I can take you to these sights in my own experience. Often, when driving around Cornwall, I will say to Don "Remember I told you about that. That is where it happened." Do not forget the ancient boundaries!

I went on to become a Sunday school teacher and by the time I was 15 my life revolved around the Church. As a family, we would find ourselves 'in Church' for some activity or other nearly every day of the week. There were prayer meetings, Bible study, choir practice, youth club on Friday, youth Bible study on a Saturday, plus 'Women's Bright Hour' which my mother led. This took place in the afternoon so I would go to Church on the way home from

School that day! Sundays meant we would be in Church three times, and once a month four times, with an after-Church rally. Once every month we had a 'Youth Squash'. This was a very social time. Lots of games, food and fun, and a special person would come and give their testimony and the epilogue.

About the same time my parents became involved with a Justice of the Peace from Plymouth named Edgar Trout. He was involved with the 'Bath Street Mission', this being a place of the famous 'Union Street' in Plymouth, where at that time there were 44 pubs in the one mile road! Edgar led a team called 'All for Christ', which consisted of various dentists, doctors and professional people from Plymouth. They would regularly be asked to visit Churches throughout our area to conduct missions and rallies. At the Bath Street Mission, on most Friday and Saturday nights, meetings were held which commenced with prayer. Then the team would go out onto the streets about 10 p.m. in the evening and bring in men and women who were just turning out of the pubs. Obviously many of these were drunk and under the influence of various drinks and drugs. The majority were sailors as Union Street was within walking distance of the naval base in Devonport. As a young teenager I would attend the meetings with my parents, but I was not allowed to actually go onto the streets with them. I can remember seeing many drunks sober up as they were given food, coffee, tea and other refreshments while listening to Edgar preach the Gospel.

One of these men was Harry Greenwood. My parents invited him to come and give his testimony at one of our Youth Squashes. He had only been 'born again' about two weeks when he came. He impacted many of our lives, even at that early part of his ministry. He joined Edgar's team and whenever in port, became a regular at his meetings. It was also during this time that we heard John Hutchison give his testimony of how God had healed him of cancer.

He owned a hotel in Devon, called 'Torbay Court'. I can remember being taken there for a Day Conference by my parents not long after we heard his testimony. Many years later John and his wife Joyce would not become just good friends, but also close partners in ministry: and a big encouragement to Don and I when we began to hear God speak to us about starting Family Camps.

Belonging to the Methodist Church there was much to be involved in at that time. Most Methodist Churches rely upon 'Local Preachers' to fill their pulpits on Sundays. This is true especially here in Cornwall where, at that time, there was an abundance of small Methodist 'chapels'. In the area I came from we had nine Churches within the five villages that joined. This did not include the Anglican and Catholic Churches. To encourage young people, there was something called the 'Mission Band', which consisted of young people who were perhaps thinking of 'ministry'. I joined. About four to six of us would go to take meetings in one of the Churches. One would pray; one gave the notices; another would sing or give testimony, and then one of the leaders of the band would preach. This was my introduction to 'ministry', all of which, now looking back, I see as God's preparation of me.

My father also became very involved in showing many Gospel films during the week in the local village Churches. Most of these films were the Billy Graham Gospel Crusade meetings, including the Rank Organization testimony films. I would often accompany my father on these visits and would be involved in praying with those who responded at the end of the meetings. My mother also became very involved in preaching, witnessing, praying, and much more.

Another incident that greatly influenced me at this time was the death of my grandmother, my mother's mother. I had been very close to her while growing up. As I have already said, we lived in close proximity. When at the age of 9 my father built a new home for us, my mother's parents also had a house built right next door to our's. My grandmother had a heart condition, which meant she was virtually bedridden. I can remember lying on her bed and having stories read to me; of peeling grapes for her and of washing her hair. When I had teeth out, I can remember lying in bed beside her as she comforted me — and many other things. Just two weeks before she died (I was now 12 -years old) my mother was tending her one day and began to talk about having a personal encounter with Jesus. This ended in my grandmother receiving Jesus as her own personal Saviour. She said to my mother, "Isn't it wonderful to know that even when you thought you were right all your life God will still accept you?" For the next two weeks I can remember a very different grandmother, one who was full of peace and faith. This left an impression upon me that God has no grand-children only children; people who have been 'born again' into His Kingdom by receiving their own personal relationship with Him as Father. You are not automatically born a Christian, nor yet a child of God, because you are born into a Christian family or a Christian nation.

Being involved in the Methodist Church and my father being the Society Steward, it was our family's job to 'host' visiting speakers. This usually meant providing a meal for them after the morning service and looking after them until the evening service. Sometimes it would mean giving them accommodation overnight on Saturday night if they came a distance. One minister, by the name of Jack Farley, came from Weston-Super-Mare. I can remember his message at the Saturday night Rally impressed me and I was 'watching' him! We had a corgi dog called *Tuppence* (in old English sterling — pounds, shillings and pence — this meant two pennies). An explanation is in order here. (My original dog was called *Penelope* but we had shortened it to *Penny!* She had a litter of puppies and we called each one after a coin. There was 'Bob' — one shilling piece; 'Florin' — two shilling piece; 'Farthing' — quarter penny piece; 'Tuppence' — two penny piece; 'Sixpence' — six penny piece; 'Crown' — two shilling and six pence, etc).

My brother and I wanted to keep a puppy so we chose *Tuppence*. On this particular Saturday she had become very ill, had bled internally and the vet did not expect her to live beyond a few hours, or at the longest a day. Before we went to Church on the Sunday morning, I passed the room where she was sleeping in her basket and saw this minister laying his hands upon her and praying for her. My curiosity was aroused! We went to Church and during the service in one of his prayers he mentioned the 'pet' at home! My, how this spoke to me! Could God, or would God do anything for my pet! When we arrived home who came running to meet us — our *Tuppence* — who was yapping and jumping around! My, God was interested in the things that concerned us — yes, even our pets! She lived many years after this, enjoying a strong, happy life. How this event influenced me can only be imagined, but I knew it did. It spoke to me that God was a God who was interested in what I was interested in. He cared for me as a whole person. He was someone I could trust to look after me.

During this time my parents became involved with the local Elim Churches at Newquay and Plymouth. We had been asked to leave the local Methodist Church because of our belief in being 'born again' and filled with the Holy Spirit, but we would not and could not keep quiet about it! Consequently my family, and about another twelve people, left the Church and began to meet in homes. When the home became too small for the amount of people, we hired the local Labour Hall to hold Church meetings in.

One year, when I was 15, the Elim Church at Newquay had a Summer Youth Camp near my home in St. Austell for one week. I can remember one evening when there was a call given for those who wanted to give their lives to the mission field to stand. I stood, very sincerely, dedicating my life to work for God. Something dramatic happened. Don't ask me to explain it, for I cannot. The only thing I know is that Jesus suddenly became real. Something within me had moved! My Christian walk with God changed. I would say that this is the time when I was 'born again'. Things certainly changed. Up until this time I read my Bible and prayed because I knew it was the right thing to do, but after that day I had a desire to read and pray. Two days later I was filled with the Holy Spirit and became so 'drunk' that I had to be helped home! Fortunately it was a Friday night and I did not have to go to College the next day, as I was still under the 'influence' all that day too!

Some weeks after this experience I became dissatisfied because I was not speaking a fluent language as I heard others doing who were filled with the Holy Spirit. At that time Harry Greenwood was with a team holding a mission in Bodmin. As a family we went along, and at the end of the meeting I responded for the Baptism in the Holy Spirit. When I went through to the prayer tent, who came to pray with me but Harry! To this day I can remember his words, "The Lord shows me that you are filled with the Holy Spirit. You just have to use what you have got." I came away from that meeting determined that I was not looking back, but going forward!

This is my second Altar of Abraham. Genesis 12, verse 8 tells us that Abraham travelled south and set up camp between Ai and Bethel. There he built an altar and worshipped the Lord. I like to call this altar the 'Altar of Intimacy'. Abraham worshipped the Lord. He called out to God. He responded to God's call to him.

Instead of waiting for God to approach him, Abraham worshipped God. There comes a time in our lives when we need to respond to God. Some—as I have already said— do this at the first altar, but for others there comes a time when we reach out to God. Being brought up in a 'Christian' environment, this second altar could be the one when things begin to 'take off' in our personal, intimate relationship with God. I know it was for me. Something had happened that proved to me that I was accepted and loved by God.

One of my biggest battles was assurance that I had been accepted by God and that I was His child. I can remember responding to many altar calls. Yes, even those for salvation, because I had no assurance. I doubted that God had accepted me and loved me. My friends were coming to Christ and having real experiences with Him, but I would look at them and doubt my own walk with God, because I had no assurance of salvation. I remember shedding my tears at many altar calls because of this lack of assurance. In my own room at home when reading my Bible and praying I would cry because I had no assurance. This lasted many years, until one day at this second altar I said within myself, 'Either I accept that God has accepted me and I live by faith, or I give everything up!' I am pleased today to be able to say that I took the first option! By faith I accepted that God accepted me and loved me. I cannot say that I immediately felt any different. I didn't. But I read the Word of God, and began to put my trust in what was written and would not allow any thoughts of doubt in this area to give me any more lack of assurance. It took time, and to this day if Satan wants to assail me, it is in this area. It is an area that I know I have taken by faith and still walk by faith in. I think this may be because, being brought up in a Christian environment, I had none of the so called 'big sins' to repent of and turn away from. Therefore, there was no dramatic overnight change in my life. In God's eyes I know that one tiny sin (in our eyes) is no different than a big sin (in our eyes). Both sent Jesus to the Cross, but in our experiences (those who would be real about it), there would appear to be a difference in our thoughts.

It was at this time that I began to call upon God and began my walk with Him. Until this time I would say it was very much experimental. Was this way of life something that I have been taught, or was it a reality that I could participate in for myself! I am sure there are many young people who, like me, have been brought up by parents who have been model disciples of Jesus, but they have yet to accept the faith, salvation and belief in the Word of God for themselves. I know most of our children went through a period of time when they had to assess for themselves who God was for them personally; that it was not just something they had been brought up with and taught, but that it had to become a reality for them.

At this altar I believe another thing takes place. Remember it tells us that Abraham pitched his tent between Bethel and Ai. (Bethel is the house of God — and Ai represents the world). Abraham set up his tent between the two. I believe this should speak to us of being able to hear and draw from God (Bethel) in order to have something to give to the world (Ai). When we really encounter God we are unable to keep it to ourselves! Like Jesus said to His disciples, "Go into the entire world and preach the Gospel" —we want to! When you are a true child of God you cannot keep the Good News (Gospel) to yourself, you have to go and share it with others. Therefore, we need the assurance of our own walk with God, and we need this second altar, with both the intimacy and the outreach joined together.

My friend and I obtained some Gospel tracts and started to witness on the streets any spare time we had! Our favourite place was one of the local harbours — Charlestown. At that time it was an active port with merchant ships in and out at regular intervals. One particular Saturday night stands out to me. Christine and I had been witnessing to some young merchant seamen. Both 16-year olds, you can image the reaction of the young men when we began to witness to them about Jesus, and giving them tracts! Christine and I finished our evening and went home to bed. We got up on Sunday and went to Church, as was our habit, and were amazed to see one of these young men in Church. At the end of the meeting he asked if he could say something. The leader of the meeting gave his permission. Then the young man told how he had made fun of us as we had witnessed to them, but during the evening he had been to the local pub, as was his habit, asked for his pint and as he brought it to his mouth a picture of Jesus appeared over it. In his words, "I threw the pint at the Landlord, ran to my digs, got on my knees and asked Jesus into my life." You can imagine how much Christine and I were agog by this. Again this was something that affected the rest of my life.

It was also during this time that my father had a real experience with God and was 'born again'. (In my book *Ouch! That Hurt* I tell how my father came to the place where he needed to forgive Hitler). Now our family was complete. My brother too was actively engaged in all that was going on, so as a family we were very much involved with the local Christian communities.

My life had been redirected because the Girls' Grammar School I attended decided that my class would no longer be taught the 'sciences'. We had three classes in my year, when usually there were only two. Because of this, my parents were told that I could leave school early because the contract had been broken that I would take a full syllabus. I had excelled in the sciences and was looking to begin a career in that realm. My father had already lined up a job for me with the local clay laboratory.

As a result, I left the Grammar School and took a 'Commercial Course' in the Technical School at Camborne. This meant that I left home around 7.30 each morning and did not get home 'till 7 p.m. because it meant a 33-mile journey every day by bus, train and then bus again. After doing half of the 3-year course I was debilitated with gastric ulcers and had to leave the course. I then began to work in an accountancy office, but I was only there for a few months because one day I was asked to do all the betting cards for the local greyhound races. I felt this was against my principles as a Christian and told my boss I would be leaving. I was able to obtain another job in a local estate agent's office, and was able to leave one job and walk into the next without being out of work. I told my parents when the episode was complete!

I really enjoyed my work in the estate agents as it was so varied. Twice a week we were involved with the cattle market as the auctioneers were my bosses. There were also farm auctions and sales to attend, plus the auction rooms for household goods, secretarial duties in the office, and writing all the cheques to pay the local farmers after the cattle markets. In all, I loved the diversity. Some days we would not know what we would be involved in until we got to work. However, I was still battling with the gastric ulcers. One day while reading my Bible, I was impressed with the verse in James 5, verse 14 about calling for the elders of the Church to pray and anoint with oil for healing. That night I went to the mid-week Bible Study and asked the Pastor to pray for me by anointing me with oil. I knew immediately that I was healed. I went out of the meeting, bought some fish and chips and ate them— something I had not been able to do for some months.

I now want to come to the third altar of Abraham. I want to call this the 'Altar of Repentance'. In Genesis 12, verses 10-20 we have the account of Abraham and his visit to Egypt. We have to acknowledge that this is one of the saddest tales of Abraham's life.

Why did he go? I believe because he did not yet have enough trust in God to sustain him and his family through the famine which was in the land. (Genesis 12:1) We know that while in Egypt Sarah obtains a maid called Hagar. As a result we have the whole episode of Ishmael and his being thrown out of the family at the age of 13. How do you think he felt? Living with his father who had trained him day in and day out, and now he had to leave his home, his father and all that he knew. You could say he was hurt! No wonder there is the hard feeling between the Arabs and the Jews today! It is a result of the dysfunctional family. Yes, a result of Abraham's lack of trust in God to sustain him and his family.

So in Genesis 12, verse 4 we find Abraham returning to the land and coming to the altar that he had built between Bethel and Ai. The Bible tells us that he again worshipped God. I believe Abraham came in repentance. He returned to the God he had first encountered there. How many times have we gone off doing our own thing just because we have not yet built the kind of trust that we need in God. We then need to come back to the place where we encountered God, and repent.

I knew somewhere along the line I had said 'sorry' to God, but saying sorry is not repenting. Don often tells this story when he is preaching about repentance: "A thief is caught in the High Street after robbing a jeweller's, and the police arresting him ask him if there is anything he wants to say. The thief says 'I'm sorry'. Of course he is sorry! He is sorry he got caught, not that he stole from the store." So often this is what happens when we pray with people for salvation. They are sorry, but with the attitude they are sorry they have been found out as being a sinner. They are not really repenting.

Repentance, as the Bible means repentance, is turning away and marching in the opposite direction. It is having a change of heart. It is knowing that it was your sin that sent Jesus to the Cross. At one time, I became very much aware that I had not truly repented. This was a number of years after the initial experience at the Camp. But I can remember the time and place where I, as an act of my will, truly repented. It was another step. It was a real experience and it made another change.

I had my 'Altar of Repentance'. This does not mean that I have never been back to this altar. I believe this is one altar that we need to be constantly returning to in order to keep all the other altars alive.

Two young men (Bryn Jones and Robert Hyssop) came to what in Cornwall is known as 'the Clay Country' to work with the Churches. They held many missions, rallies and various meetings in many of the Methodist Churches. As a family we attended.

It was also at this time that a young man one day knocked on our door looking for his friend who was then Pastor of our young Church. Being the night of our mid-week Bible Study, my father asked him to take the meeting. He preached a message from John 14, 'If you love Me, keep My commandments'. Throughout the whole message I could only hear one thing—'You know what I have asked of you. Now keep my commandment.' I cannot remember anything else that was spoken that evening other than the words God had put in my heart. Next morning I went to work and gave a two-week notice, then came home and told my parents!

We now come to my fourth altar of Abraham. Taking ownership of what God has given you and called you to. Genesis 13, verses 17-18 say *Take a walk in every direction and explore the new possessions I am giving you. Abraham moved his camp to the oaks of Mamre, which is at Hebron, and there he built an altar to the Lord.*

In particular I FELT God was calling me to the 'ministry of helps' recorded in Corinthians. (More of this later). It was at this time I took possession of what, for about 18 months, I had heard God talking to me about— full-time service for Him.

The name of that young man who came to our Bible Study that night was DON DOUBLE! Yes, just three years later I changed my name to Mrs. Double.

Don stayed on a few days and then moved on to his next mission, and I worked out my two week's notice period and left my job. With my last wage packet, just £5.00 for a whole week, I bought myself a suitcase, because somehow I thought God would have me travelling! About two weeks later our friends had a call from Don to say he had a mission on and some of those who were going to help him could not go and he asked Arthur if he and his wife could go to help him.

One evening my father said to me, "You have not heard from Edgar yet about joining his team. Why don't you go up with Arthur and Joy and help with the mission." So it was decided I would join Arthur and Joy for a three-week visit to Bury St. Edmunds, Suffolk to help with the mission. Just two days before we were due to go my father suggested that my Mum also join us as she had had a busy summer. At this time she was taking in guests from Easter 'till September each year, and it would give her a break. So, the four of us set off for Suffolk. Up until this time I had only been out of Devon and Cornwall a couple of times, so this was somewhat of an adventure for me.

I had no idea how in a few weeks my life would once again take a radical change of direction. While working with Don and his associates I received a letter from Edgar Trout saying that he was sure God had called me to work full-time, but it was not with his team but with a 'like-minded' team. I did not need God to write it in the sky, for I was already working with a 'like-minded' team; a team who were called to evangelize. So I told my parents that I would not be returning to Cornwall for a while as I was staying in Suffolk to work with what was then called 'Miracle Revivals'. I was filling a role in the team that no one else could. Having been trained in secretarial and accountancy work, I was immediately thrust into this area of work in the team. Now I began to see how the change that had taken place in our school life was God's purpose for me. What good would 'the sciences' have been to me! Instead I had the skills needed to help administrate the team.

(Don's own testimony confirms just how necessary this was as, because of childhood sickness; when I met him he was very unlearned and still very uncertain of himself when communicating with 'business people', especially if it would mean he might have to write. As he was not able to spell, it soon became my job to communicate with all the necessary authorities when requesting permission for meetings, booking halls, etc.)

One of the first things I was asked to do was to produce a newsletter. All we had was an old flat-bed copier. It is difficult to explain how this piece of equipment worked in today's automatic society, but it consisted of a bed of ink upon which was laid a mesh. A stencil was cut on the typewriter, which was then placed on the mesh and each piece of paper was then placed onto the stencil and a roller rolled over the page. (We still have some of the first newsletters we produced in this way).

It was not long before we had so many contacts who wanted the newsletters we had to believe God to have it printed professionally. I then began to keep account of the money coming in and out. This book we still have, and only recently Don and I were looking at it and seeing how in the first year of keeping records we had a turnover of just £800! Not much in today's society, but in those days it was quite a considerable amount.

We were trusting God to supply all we needed for living and to run the ministry. Many people call it 'living by faith'. But the Bible tells us that 'the just shall live by faith.' So, in fact, every child of God lives by faith. We were in the position that we had no visible sign of support, so we were trusting God to speak to His people to support us. This is the way we have lived for the past 45 years and we would like to testify today that God has never let us down. He has always supplied. Although at times He has cut it mighty fine, we have never been in the position that we had a bill that we were unable to pay. God is faithful. Those He calls He also equips and provides for.

When I first heard God call me I felt He was calling me to the 'ministry of helps'. We find this in 1 Corinthians 12, verse 28. I don't know where I got it from, but I had this idea that if God had called me to be a 'help' then whatever I was asked to do, as long as it was within His purpose for my life, I would be able to do it! Many times I would be asked to do something which I had never done before. Some things I had no idea how to do, but I would turn my heart to God and believe for His enabling—and then do it! I often became nervous and had 'butterflies' in my stomach, but God was faithful and never let me down. All these years later I look at the path Don and I have trod and there is hardly a job within team life that I have not done at some stage in our ministry.

Abraham's fifth altar was his final altar. I call this the 'Altar of Sacrifice'. (Genesis 22) God did not want Isaac's body. What He really wanted was Abraham's heart. I think Abraham has become very much involved with the gift and the promise of God. Here he was with his son Isaac that God had promised him. He was growing up and becoming a man and suddenly God asks Abraham to sacrifice him. This was totally against all that Abraham knew of God. God did not require human sacrifices like other cultures around him, but in sheer obedience Abraham obeys and goes to Mount Moriah to sacrifice his son. We all know what happens. God provides the sacrifice (a ram caught in the thicket) and gives Isaac back to Abraham.

Don and the team, of which I was now a part, were involved in a mission in Blythe, Northumberland. We were engaged and just a couple of months from marriage.

Every mission we have, we always include a missionary (overseas) thrust, because we feel this is something God wants us to do. This mission, being one of the very early ones where we were learning 'on the job' as it were, we had obtained a film from a couple called M.A. Daoud, who had very successful mission. God spoke to us, and we ended up at the altar in the Church committing ourselves—that together or apart—we would serve the Lord for the rest of our lives. That day I put my Isaac (Don) on the altar. He was no longer mine, but God's. I really did not know how powerful this action would become over the years when I had to stay home and look after the family, with Don going away for three to four weeks at a time. I never once felt God had taken my husband from me. He couldn't, because I had laid him on the altar and he was first and foremost God's. Anytime he was home with us as a family, and any time we spent together, was God saying He loved me and giving me time with Don.

How different our lives would have been if this had not been a reality. Sacrifice is something that none of us really like or enjoy, but when it comes from your heart relationship with God it is not a burden, or anything else, but a joy that gives you a relationship with the Lord that deepens as the sacrifice becomes a reality in our lives.

One of the early team members was a man, who was affectionately named 'Pop' by everyone. He was in his 80's but travelled with us on the missions, conferences, and conventions, and he played the piano for the praise and worship in our meetings. I owe a lot to him for all the input he gave into my life in those early years. He instilled in me a faith to believe God for every aspect of my life. One story that sticks out as a land mark in my life involving 'Pop' was the day when he called early in the morning to say that his wife had been taken seriously sick, and he would not be able to come to the mission that was starting that very evening. We had no one to play. What were we going to do!

At the age of 9 I had taken a few piano lessons for a few months, but had not accomplished anything really profitable. I had done a lot of choir work while in the Methodist Church in my early teens, and had a little knowledge of the music score, notes, rests, etc. By the time I met Don I was playing the guitar a little, the accordion and a portable organ, but all this was for my own enjoyment and I had no 'vision' for anything else. Also I had no 'ear' for music. All I knew was how to read the melody line and which notes they were on the piano! Don knew this, and in the middle of the day sat me on the organ stool. By this time we had a portable reed organ. He laid his hands on me and prayed, believing that I would be able to play the songs for the meeting that night! God did it! I sat at the organ and worked out the songs for the meeting. Those of you who knew us in the 60's and early 70's will remember that I played for all our meetings during those years.

While we were at a mission in Ampthill, Bedfordshire, Don and I were invited by the Salvation Army Corps leader to have a meal at his home. During the time with him he turned to Don and said, "Do you know why I come to the meetings every evening?" Don says he thought he was going to say to hear him preach the Word, but instead he said "to hear your wife play the organ!" I nearly fainted. Here was the leader of one of the top Salvation Army Corps in the country, which had a very accomplished Band and choir, saying he came to hear me play! If nothing else it made me realize just what God had done for me.

In 1972 I was pregnant with our son, Joel, and at about seven months Don said to me one day "you are not sitting on that stool playing for the meetings any more, it is too uncomfortable for you". I was very large. Joel was 9lb 8ozs at birth! At that time Julia (our oldest daughter) was a very accomplished pianist, having taken up music from the age of five. God had given her a gift as a very young girl. We could sing a song to her and she would go straight to the piano and play it—note perfect! So Don said "Julia can play for the meetings," and in fact I have not played an instrument since! If you have never heard me speak about it, I am a big believer in the fact that we go through seasons in our life, and this was one of those 'seasons' for me. I had fulfilled the purpose of God for me at that time. I had been a 'help' and now it was time to pass on to another stage.

As many of you will know, I am Don's second wife. (More about this will come in Don's side of the story). Don was given custody of the two children from that first marriage. When Don and I were married, Nigel was eight years old and Julia five years old. Because they had settled well with Don's parents (for Don and the children moved back to live with his parents when his marriage broke up) we felt it best for them to continue schooling in Hadleigh with his parents while we continued in ministry, and at holiday times they would travel with us, and wherever we were they could be. At this time we had no home of our own so it was a more settled environment for them.

When Nigel was 15 (he was the last year to leave school at the age of 15 here in the UK), he decided that he wanted to come to Cornwall to live with us. One day when we arrived home to spend time with them he made his announcement. "When I leave school in June I am coming to Cornwall to live with you!" Julia quickly butted in and said, "So am I." Both Don and I were thrilled because we wanted this decision to be theirs and not something forced on them.

This was going to mean a lot of adjustments for me personally. Nigel would start an apprenticeship at a printer's, and Julia would enter the local Secondary School. This would mean I would not be free to travel with Don. Although Stephen by this time was four years old and we were looking at his first school, we had taken him

everywhere. It would not be unusual to come to a meeting
and see Stephen asleep in a travel cot at the back of the
meeting while Don and I were ministering, Don preaching
and me leading the praise and worship!

One mission stands out in my memory. We were in the
local cinema in Helston, Cornwall, and I had a
metal-framed folding cot that we had brought home from
Denmark with us. At that time we had nothing like this
here. I would dress him in night clothes, put a coat on him
and at the beginning of the meeting put him in the cot
between the back of two rows of seats. He would sit there
and watch the proceedings, usually until about 7.45 p.m.
Then, as I was in the middle of leading a song, or maybe
singing a solo, I would see a little head pop up. He'd give
me a wave and that would signal he was going to sleep.
And sleep he did! Then at the end of the meeting we would
lift him out of the cot, take him back to where we were
staying, plant him in his bed and hear nothing from him
until the next morning. This was his life up until he started
school. It did not matter what venue the meeting was in,
when he was ready to sleep he would sleep! On the floor—
stretched out on a couple of chairs—or wherever!

Soon after Nigel made his announcement, Don and I
were in a ministers' retreat with Jean and Elmer Darnell.
Jean knew nothing about what had happened but while
praying over me she said "God has given you something to
look after for Him." There was no need to tell me what this
meant—Nigel and Julia. They were God's gifts to me.
Those around us in those early years will know how much
I would not travel with Don unless the children could come
with us. This was until the day Julia got married. A couple
of days after I said to Don, "I don't know why but I now
feel free to travel with you again, wherever you need me!"
So it happened, when Don needed me I travelled with him.
God graciously gave us a wonderful 'mother's help' who
came to live in with us, and whenever I needed to be away

with Don she would care for Stephen, Joel and Faith, plus the others we had living with us. Over the years we had many young people living in our home. Some came to be trained in ministry, and some came to be part of our family through various avenues. Some of them lived with us for many years. The longest being nine years; others for lesser times.

With Don travelling away so much (sometimes when he went overseas he would be away for four to six weeks), I would be at home with the family. One could say at these times I lived as a 'single parent', but I never felt that because we had strong friendships and commitments in our Church that supported me. The children always knew I could call in any of the elders of the Church if I had a problem which I could not solve. I think I only had to do that once. They then realized that they could not 'get away' with things because Dad was away!

As most of you will know, Don is six foot six inches tall —and I am only five foot three inches! All of our children have followed Don in their stature, and by the time our boys were eleven they were taller than me!

Heather's own story ends somewhat abruptly here as she was not able to complete it before leaving us on her journey 'home'!

It is now my joy and great privilege, along with Don, to bring together many other things from the legacy which Heather has left that will help to complete her life's story.

Gwen Macmillan

2

A Precious Daughter

At Heather's Thanksgiving Services, both in St Austell and Taunton, I paid tribute to a very special lady who, in a very real way, enabled me to have the best wife in the world (for me, that is)—a fact that I have sought to declare constantly throughout the 43 years of our married life wherever I have been teaching and preaching. That lady is, of course **Rhoda Martin**—*Heather's mother. I want to honour her for every way she trained Heather up in the ways of the Lord to become the multi-faceted godly wife that she was to me. So now as we reflect on Heather's wonderful life, I am thrilled to invite Rhoda to tell us something of her own story through—'A Precious Daughter'.*

What wonderful sounds rang in our ears in the late afternoon on 20th May 1944 when those attending me announced "Mrs. Martin, you have a baby daughter." We already had a son Brian, born in March 1941, and now as I took this brand new little life into my arms I knew I was holding the one I had dedicated to God as I carried her in my womb. Heather Rhoda, a treasured gift from God. I was filled with a mixture of joy at seeing this new little life before me—a life to love and nurture—and the awesome responsibility of now caring for two little ones.

My husband John and I were both raised in families who were regular Church members and we were married in July 1939, just two months before World War II broke out. John, who served in the Royal Navy, spent long periods away from home (especially during the war years) which meant that I needed to take the main responsibility of raising the children.

Although the Christian parentage we had been given had provided a good foundation in our lives, we were at that time more 'nominal' than committed Christians, for we were not 'born again,' but when John left to go to serve in the war we covenanted together that wherever he was in the world at 9 pm. each evening we would read our Bibles and pray. This promise meant a lot to me as I was at home alone with the children, and I knew the Lord heard those prayers and honoured the establishing of this commitment. Through my own upbringing Church going was always a regular part of my life, so I used to take the children with me as babies.

John did not complete his naval career until 1948, and then on returning home he had to have a further period of two and a half years in hospital for medical treatment. This meant that the children hardly saw their Dad, which was hard for us all. Whilst I sought to 'hold the family fort' so to speak, and to bring a measure of security and stability of 'family life', as a loving Mum raising the children single-handedly, I knew I could never totally be a Mum and a Dad. So it was not until 1951 that Brian and Heather really knew what it was to have a father at home, and some adjustment to 'family life' could begin and develop. With many of our families living very near to us we sought to enjoy the newness of being a 'whole family' with them too, and life began to regain some measure of normality after all those years apart.

Family time

As a child Heather loved to climb on her bicycle and go out for rides exploring the countryside around. With Cornwall being such a beautiful part of the country she spent many happy hours enjoying her adventures, although it was probably the bike she appreciated most at that time rather than the scenery! *That real appreciation came later!* Being so near the coast too she always enjoyed our regular trips to the beaches. In fact John and I took Brian and Heather out as often as we could after he came home. I guess we were trying to make up for all the years we had had to spend apart during their very young lives. Perhaps the added excitement of those times was when the children would ask, 'Where are we going today?' Dad's answer would usually be "Guess!" The route he took did not usually give much of a clue of the final destination as he would try and fool the children by going a different way to get to a familiar place. This all added to the fun of those times out together and helped to teach the children to be quite observant of things and places.

Heather loved those trips out together, especially to the coastal places nearby, seeing them as opportunities to have fun and explore! And explore she did with her brother and cousin. They were like three lads together! In fact anything we sought to do as a 'family' understandably the children loved. Heather cherished the fact that it was her Dad who taught her to swim. Always a great achievement; made all the more special when you've done it with Dad!

Picnics were another great favourite whenever we went out together, because it was more than just an opportunity to eat out doors, it was the fun we sought to enjoy together too. I remember the time when John made a 'rope swing' across the river and he, of course, had to test it out before he allowed Brian and Heather to use it. Just as well that he did as he landed right in the middle of the river up to his knees! Taking spare clothes for the children was normal when packing up the car for our outings, but from then on I had to remember to take spare clothes for John too!

John was not one to voice his deep feelings and emotions easily, but the children were nonetheless aware of his deep affection for them through the things he so readily did and the way he treated them, which so clearly showed his love for them. The hand-made toys crafted so lovingly for the children were much cherished, and Heather herself voiced expression of this in the tribute she gave at her Dad's funeral service. Also the hard work he put into building a home for Don and Heather; undertaking the whole of the construction work on the bungalow himself. His expressions of love went far deeper than words and far beyond our own family too. It meant so much to Heather to see the fondness he had for the grand-children—and they too of him.

As many of you will know, Heather had a great love of history. Perhaps this was helped by her eagerness to ask questions and to listen to some of the brave things that John did through his War years. Despite the fact that, as a young child, Heather saw so little of her Dad whilst he was serving the King and country, in her eyes he did become one of her greatest childhood heroes. War is ugly, we know, but Heather was so proud of her Dad's achievements in saving lives; something which he also did the day of the famous floods in Lynton and Lynmouth in Devon.

As Heather grew up, and went on to her own marriage and family life (and even ministry), she held on to two of the greater things that she said her Dad taught her about life. They were 'hard work never hurt anyone,' and 'in whatever you do have fun and enjoy yourself,' and she certainly became a hard-worker and one who never lost her sense of fun either!

Penny and *Tuppence,* two little Corgi dogs, became part of our family, too, as the children were keen to have a pet. Heather loved them and I can vividly remember her playing with them for hours on end, even at times dressing them up like dolls and taking them for walks in her pram! They must have loved her too, and been very tolerant, as I can never remember them objecting in any nasty way.

Another thing Heather loved was music and singing, so for a while she was able to have some piano lessons. Not for very long though, but again long enough for God to be able to take and use later on in her life. She had a lovely singing voice too and her joyful songs always used to resound around the home and wherever else she had opportunity to sing out God's praises. Her musical gifts have been such a blessing to countless people.

I used to pray a lot with the children and seek to teach them how to both talk and listen to God. It was such a natural part of our lives together. When Heather was nearing the end of her Primary School days she so wanted to move on to the Grammar School but had been told that she would never be able to pass her necessary 11 Plus examination. But Heather being Heather did not let these comments hinder her hearts desire, so she got on her knees and prayed! God heard that simple and sincere prayer of faith and to Heather's delight when the day came for the results to be announced to the whole school, her name was the first one to be called. We were so proud of her and she was so encouraged in her faith as it was her first specific answer to a BIG prayer!

Changing times lead to growing times

When Heather was nine years old I had a real and deep encounter with the Living God. He so changed my life that it had a big impact on the whole family, especially Heather, although it was several years later before John came to that place of total commitment too.

Heather's own decision to commit her life to the Lord Jesus Christ at the age of nine was real and sincere, and she was always keen for the opportunity to come with me to every meeting she could. In fact anywhere that would enable her to learn more about God and to see what He was doing, she was eager to be there! Heather witnessed many miracles in those early days and she grew hungry to know more of His power and reality in her own young life. At home she was always eager to read her Bible and pray and I could see so clearly that God was shaping her life in His hands. Her involvement in Sunday school teaching, Church youth club activities, choir, Bible studies, prayer meetings, youth club . . . and helping in any other areas of service in the Church she could, was the growing desire of her heart. In fact all she ever wanted to do was to do the Lord's will—and to love and follow Him.

As a Mum I saw it as my responsibility to train her as a daughter in whatever I was doing, whether that be cooking, embroidery, dressmaking or jobs around the house. Heather enjoyed knitting, all types of sewing, crochet, embroidery, reading, writing, cooking, cleaning, gardening . . . or helping to repair her bike—even the engine of the car! She loved those times together as mother and daughter, because I never pushed her aside by giving her the impression that I could do jobs quicker on my own. Nor did I expect her to be perfect, but I sought instead to allow her to come alongside to learn, and make mistakes! The opportunity to help teach her so many basic skills was a special part of our home life, and I often recall memories of those shared times; and realize now just how important that training proved to be as Heather went on to serve God as a wife, mother and 'homemaker', as well as in her wider ministry.

Caring for others, either in our home or reaching out

to them from our home, was such a natural part our life together as a family, so Heather's heart soon became sensitive to the needs of others and she learned to give to them what they needed. If we had what they didn't have, she wanted to be involved in anything we could do to give or share with them. That generous heart, I know, went on giving right up to the end.

By the time Heather moved from school to college and then out into the work place she had development an immovable faith in God and would not compromise her Christian principles. In fact in order not to do that, she made the decision to leave her first job in an accountancy office and God provided her with another one straight away in an Estate Agent's office; a work she so enjoyed. Again we saw a woman of strength in the making, because even when she faced obstacles and struggles along the way, she saw them as challenges and opportunities to trust Him more and to prove His power.

From a very young age, books were a delight to Heather. She just loved reading—and writing. Little did I know then that she would go on to write a number of her own books; books which would help and inspire so many all over the world. Or that the daughter who was always so keen to study her Bible and serve in the smallest of ways would go on to teach, preach and minister so mightily in this nation and overseas.

John and I were privileged to witness Heather's first introduction to Don, this young evangelist who had arrived 'out of the blue' at our door, having travelled from East Anglia, in search of a young pastor friend. It's strange how God unfolds His plans sometimes, isn't it! Being the night of our mid-week meeting at the Church, John asked him to stay and take that meeting. The message he preached from John 14 so impacted Heather and she knew that God was again leading her into new steps of faith. From that moment she never looked back but sought only to follow Him in obedience and trust.

It soon became clear to us all that God had appointed for Don and Heather's paths to meet and that he had plans for their future together. And so it was that two years later we had the joy of seeing them set out on that journey in God together as husband and wife. Right from a little child God had birthed in her heart the desire to serve Him, and all we ever wanted to do was to help train her up and encourage her to simply do His will, whatever or wherever that was.

Working together

It was a real joy to be able to actively show our support to both Don and Heather as they walked this new path of faith together by serving with them in the early days of their meetings and missions around the country. This involved us all in every form of ministry together, from the very many practical areas of service that needed to be done, to the more spiritual aspects. But we soon learned that every aspect is important as we serve the Lord, and whatever we needed to do we did 'as unto Him.' He honoured that by His presence and blessing. We learned a lot together in those days about working together as a 'team'.

I was able to continue my involvement with them in this way for a number of years, both at home and abroad, and together we witnessed many miracles of God's healing love and power at work in lives so in need of His touch. Over the years that active involvement with them 'out on the job', so to speak, obviously changed, but I remained an active prayer partner with them. I have so many lovely memories of our working through each one of those 'seasons' together.

Sacrificial love

Heather has always been such a loyal and loving

daughter to me over the years and I have so appreciated every way that she has continued to be there for me in my own times of need, especially since her Dad died. The love and care that both Don and Heather have expressed to me has so many times been very sacrificial to them, I know, but they didn't hold back.

Time together in their home with the family, and their visits and phone calls to me, have always meant so much. Even with their full lives I have always known that I belonged and that I was not alone. Their loving hearts have always wanted to make sure that I was alright and had everything I needed, especially if they were going away. In between their busy lives of travelling, they took me shopping and other places that I needed to go; nothing was ever too much trouble for them. Dear Heather even took me to doctor's or hospital appointments in between her own when her own health was declining. Such love! She always thought of others before herself, even along the toughest path.

When Heather had to face her battle with cancer, I found it a very hard trial to walk through as her mother, watching her suffer as she did. Naturally, like Heather herself and many others, I believed all the way along her journey of battling with declining health that the Lord was going to raise her up and undertake for her and there were moments when we saw real evidence of His healing. On one such occasion a friend and I had been praying earnestly one evening for Heather's health, realizing that she was in great discomfort through a build-up of fluid on her lungs and was battling for breath. The next morning when I went up to visit her in the hospital she was sitting in a chair knitting a cardigan for Don. What a change! The doctor's had been able to drain her lungs and she was able to breath. That time was special as I knew God had heard those prayers.

It was hard when more fluid then started to build up in her stomach again; it was as though her whole body was being attacked. This time, although I was praying those same earnest prayers, there was not the same evidence of healing. Instead, although her faith and spirit remained strong, I was seeing her body become increasingly weak and her heart was ready to accept whatever Father wanted, whether it was healing now or back home with Him in Heaven, where our new bodies are not subject to pain and suffering. It was clear that she was at peace in her spirit and that she was ready to meet Him.

Time to go Home

I guess no parent ever thinks that their children are going to die before them, so it is not an easy thing to face, especially with a daughter whose heart was so set on serving Him. But I know that we are committed to a loving God who has promised *Never to leave us or forsake us*, (Hebrews 13:5) least of all in the tough times when we need Him so much. Our times are in His hands and in His tender care and I know that through every part of Heather's journey with Him He kept that personal promise, even along her final path of suffering. Her body may have become sick and weak but His very presence and enabling kept her strong in faith and trust right to the end.

I am so grateful for all those who cared so tenderly for Heather during her times in the hospitals and the Hospice, and for the loving support of the family and many friends.

As her Mum I found that so comforting, when I felt I could do so little other than to just be there for her. And I thank God for a wonderful daughter who has shown me so much more about her Lord and Saviour than I could ever have taught her. One day I know I will see her again in Heaven where we will enjoy life in His presence together— for ever!

The investment of time, attention and energy in the lives of our children is a great God-given privilege. It is never a waste of time!

- 3 -

A Devoted Wife

A wife of noble character who can find?
She is worth far more than rubies.
Proverbs 31:10

It was a beautiful sunny day in Cornwall on Saturday 9th May 1964 when Heather and I were married at Leek Seed Methodist Church in St. Austell at 11.00 a.m. I arrived at the Church with my best man Tony Holloway, a very good friend, and we, along with our families and friends who had gathered to share that day with us, eagerly waited the arrival of Heather and her three bridesmaids: my daughter Julia, Heather's cousin Julie and a Danish friend, Jetta.

Some time previous we had met and befriended Captain Brian Eastwell, a Salvation Army Officer, and we soon learned that God had a plan in linking our lives together! By his own admission, Brian's Christian faith had become very 'dry' so we invited him along to one of our Easter Conventions. What a fresh encounter that proved to be for Brian, for it was there that he met with God again and was wonderfully baptized in the Holy Spirit. Needless to say he was totally transformed and it was the start of a new life and ministry as the Holy Spirit invaded every part of his being, filling him to overflowing. We became great friends, so it was a real joy to Heather and I that Brian was able to conduct our wedding.

As you will have already read in 'Heather's story' (*notes which she personally wrote and which are used in the first chapter of this book*), we had known our own individual and personal 'call' to serve the Lord in the days leading up to our wedding, but now the day had arrived when we were taking our wedding vows and entering into a marriage covenant together; a covenant which would both seal those promises and release us into what God had planned for our 'togetherness' in Him. Proverbs 18, verse 22 says *He who finds a wife finds what is good* and as we walked down the aisle together, I sensed it was not me who had found a good thing, but that God had got there before me and chosen a good wife for me! What a precious day it was as we stepped out into a whole new future together.

After our reception with friends and family we travelled over to the lovely Isles of Scilly where we spent our honeymoon. It was here where we were to undertake our first 'mission' work together as Mr. and Mrs. Double! I had previously written a Gospel tract, entitled "That Certain Void", and Heather and I had as our goal to put a copy of this in everyone's door, including that of the then Prime Minister, Harold Wilson, who had a house on the Island. What joy we had in fulfilling that goal!

Heather, as a person, was naturally quite shy and reserved and although she had a big heart for people she also enjoyed her own company. Yet, even with that disposition, she never ever used it as an excuse for not stepping out into new things, for she knew that when God calls He always equips and enables. She was an 'over-comer' and her constant testimony to the glory of God was "in what He has given me to do I am not shy" — and she wasn't! Her open confession of that fact brought increasing release and freedom into new and greater things.

From the moment I met Heather I knew she had a big open heart for God and in my role for her as her husband, I had a desire to help and encourage her in every way to fulfil all that was on His heart for her. The more I realized how generous God had been with His giftings to her, the more I realized the responsibility I had to generously love her in obedience to His instructions in Ephesians 5, verse 25: *Husbands, love your wives, just as Christ loved the Church and gave himself up for her . . .* It's an instruction that no man can possibly fulfil without reliance on His strength and enabling.

Several years back there was a book written by F. LaGard Smith, entitled, *Men of Strength for Women of God*, which challenged us men into helping to develop and encourage 'women of God'. I was so aware that I had been entrusted with a great 'women of God' in Heather and my desire to be a 'man of strength' for her certainly kept me on my toes in God!

It was hard for me in the time available at Heather's Thanksgiving Services, both in Cornwall and at the GNC Summer Camp in Taunton, to try to squeeze into a 'nutshell' aspects of Heather's multi-faceted life which would bring an adequate tribute to her as a woman of God —and as my cherished wife. Perhaps this is why there was little wonder when so many of us quite independently used verses from Proverbs 31 in bringing tribute to her, as it is a passage which many have said has Heather's name written all over it!

A lifestyle of Worship

First and foremost Heather was a child of God, and as she sought to live out her surrendered life, she knew that above everything her own personal relationship with her Heavenly Father was paramount. As a true worshipper she desired to give God everything, for she wanted her life to count. She delighted in entering into that holy place where she could be alone with Father and express her love to Him by sitting at His feet in prayer, whether in silent adoration, in song or in those quiet personal whispers of the heart to each other. Heather knew she could only give to others from the overflow of her own supply, so that intimacy was something she cherished and guarded, whilst still embracing a lifestyle of worship.

Under God I knew that I was Heather's 'number one' and she made sure that nothing or no-one came between us —not even our children. She knew that the greatest way we could show our love to them and build security for them was by our own oneness as parents in the harmony, friendship and relationship we had with each other. Heather also knew that the closer we came to God the closer we would be to each other, and we proved this to be so true.

It has to be said, though, that in our own marriage it took time and some hard work to us to get to this place of open communication with each other. We had been married for about ten years and had a good marriage. But, as the saying goes, 'good is the enemy of the best' and we didn't want just a good marriage. We wanted the best!

On one occasion we were driving together to Penzance, where I had been invited to speak at a Church event. We began to talk as we drove along and our conversation became very 'real' about our communication with each other. I began to share with Heather how I couldn't be totally open with her for fear of her reactions and very soon I discovered that Heather felt the same way, because she was afraid of my reactions.

The conversation we had on the way to Penzance that day was a difficult one to face, but the fruit was wonderful! It proved to be a real water-shed in our marriage, because we could then face and deal with the issues which were blocking open communication with each other. A 'bridge' of total trust began to be built; one which could take a greater weight load than the fragile one that had been there before. We knew that whatever we needed to drive over that 'bridge' in order to be open with each other, there would be strength and security to become closer to each other. We proved this to be so true. Our relationship and love for each other was certainly deepened and strengthened and became very real to us as we journeyed on together in our marriage. It is so liberating when the Lord shines His light into the shadows of those hidden corners of our lives and casts out all fear.

It is a wonderful thing when husbands and wives become their own best friends. Heather and I certainly enjoyed this aspect of our relationship and we endeavoured to do everything we could together. 'Partner' has become a word which the world has not only stolen, but also distorted its meaning. Therefore, when we talk about our 'partnership' together, as husband and wife and as best friends, something of the beauty of that relationship seems lost in the words in today's world. That's sad when even the dictionaries describe partner as 'sharers'—and as husbands and wives.

In Genesis 12 we read of how God spoke to Abraham and of the promises He made. But as Sarah was part of Abraham she was also part of God's call on her husband's life, and he could not have fulfilled God's promised covenant without her. Likewise we always saw that what God had given to us as husband and wife was to bring fulfilment of His promises to us and through us. To bring completing not competing, and Heather always sought to emphasize this fact whenever she was teaching on marriage. "We were made to compliment our husband, to add to him . . . We both have something that the other does not have . . . Our husband is incomplete without us . . . God has given us the ability to be to our husband what he needs us to be," were all highlighted in her notes! Not because she saw me as hopelessly inadequate, but because she saw how much greater both of us could be as we brought 'completion' to each other. For when both partners bring their natural and spiritual gifts into the marriage there is a complementing of each other, and in that union they have everything they need for a wonderful partnership.

Heather knew that God's first call on her life was that of a 'helper,' one who would bring support, and how I appreciated the way she ministered to me throughout the years of our marriage. When she knew I was taking new steps in God she was the first to pray for me and to find ways to express her support and help, even in the affirming eye-contact she sought to keep with me as I was preaching. Her heart was always to encourage faith, to build up, to honour, to appreciate and to love, even in the most practical ways. I will always remember early in our marriage at a 'Leaders' Conference' when a well-recognized lady came up to me and said 'Your new wife is really good'. "Why do you say that?" I said. Her reply was, "In Proverbs 31 it says 'her husband is respected at the City gate where he takes his seat among the elders of the land'. I love the way she irons your shirts. You look very smart." This was only a small thing really, but Heather honoured me, and it was noticed by others too.

In God's call on my life I knew that Heather was not only a hundred per cent behind me but also a hundred per cent alongside. We were a team and whether that meant that Heather stayed at home to care for the family, or that she travelled with me in ministry, we were one. In Proverbs 31:11 we read, "Her husband can trust her and he will be greatly enriched in his life." I could trust Heather anywhere and with anything and this became very real to me following our conversation on the road to Penzance, which I referred to earlier. She was a brilliant listener too, and I knew that I could trust her with the deepest secrets of my heart, my emotions, my disappointments, and my fears, as well as my hopes and joys. I could always be myself and totally real with her and I knew she would be totally real and honest with me too. That openness was very precious and brought us both such freedom and confidence in each other.

As many of you will agree, Heather was a very strong woman, but one with a gentle and quiet spirit born out of her submission; firstly to God and then to me as the husband He had given her. A truly beautiful heart attitude! We talked very openly and honestly with each other on issues we faced and we always respected each other's opinions, but when a decision had to be made Heather was glad to leave that responsibility with me. I have to say that the decisions I made didn't always prove to be the best ones, but I can't ever remember a time when Heather came back and pointed a finger at me saying "I told you so." I so appreciated her godly character and wisdom.

Her teaching was always firmly based on God's Word. At every opportunity Heather lived in God's Word, so the application of its truth and teaching flowed naturally from her. It was sound and it was practical, for she desired not only to present truth but to help people in its application. Titus 2 speaks of 'The importance of older women of God teaching what is good' and of 'Training the younger women to love their husbands,' and Heather cherished every opportunity to plant that 'seed Truth' into the hearts of others younger in the faith. She wanted to see their marriages blossom and be honouring to Him. Her ministry bore much fruit, because that is how she sought to live as my wife. There was never any credibility gap between what she taught and how she lived.

A love for all times

Heather and I shared a loving marriage relationship—built on the Word of God. On the 9th May 1964, when we exchanged our 'Marriage Vows', we entered into a covenant with each other before God and people, a covenant which was more than just words. We promised to love each other **at all times**. That meant even when we didn't see the best in each other; when old habits irritated; when circumstances were tough; in sickness and in health, we were still committed to love and cherish each other. For we knew that that which bound us together in marriage was not just our own love for each other, but it was our personal and united love for the Lord Jesus Christ. Only His love enabled us to be patient and kind to each other; not demanding our own way or holding grudges. Only His love enabled us to hardly notice when we got things wrong, to always believe in each other, and to stand our ground in defending each other, as we are so clearly taught in 1 Corinthians 13.

Ecclesiastes 4, verse 12 speaks of the strength of a 'three-stranded cord which is not easily broken.' Why a three-stranded cord? Heather was always one who wanted to research and explore things in greater depth in order to bring a richer understanding, so she talked with a local chandler about the construction and qualities of the various ropes and cords which he created. It was fascinating to discover that the three-stranded cord is, in fact, the strongest construction of all! For us it represented Heather's and my life being woven together in a living relationship with the Lord Jesus. It was such a simple illustration, yet one which is key to the strength of any marriage, and certainly a fact that we emphasized in our teaching together around the world.

We had the joy of celebrating 43 years of marriage together and those celebrations were not just something we limited to the anniversary date of our Wedding Day each year, but as often as possible throughout the year too! This is something that we have encouraged many hundreds of couples to do too as we have led 'Married

Couples Seminars' together over the years, so I hope there
are lots of celebrations still happening all around the
world! Sadly in today's world, marriage is not given the
honour that God intended and the preciousness of entering
into covenant together before God means so little to many.
How I thank God for the privilege that Heather and I had
to help couples build some strong foundations into their
marriages, according to *Heaven's Blueprint!* (Don and
Heather's book on Marriage.)

Sometimes we planned our Wedding Anniversaries
together, but at other times some secret planning went on
behind the scenes! One such occasion was our 21st
Wedding Anniversary which I arranged as a surprise for
Heather. Having driven to Plymouth we then boarded a
plane for Heathrow. Lunch had been arranged at '90 Park
Lane', one of the best restaurants in the West End at that
time, and in the evening I had booked for Heather and I to
go to see 'Starlight Express'. After staying the night in a
lovely hotel in London, we headed back to the airport and
boarded a flight back home. It wasn't easy for me to get
away with surprises very often, but this time Heather had
no idea and we had a wonderful time of celebration.

For our Ruby Wedding Anniversary just three years
before Heather died, we were able to combine this
celebration with my 70th and Heather's 60th birthdays.
This time we had planned everything together, as we
wanted to share this time with our family and as many
treasured friends as possible. Heather did a grand job in
handling all the organization for this very joyous occasion
at Alverton Manor in Truro and the Lord answered our
prayers by giving us a beautiful day in equally beautiful
surroundings. As part of our celebrations we had written
our own personal 'anniversary vows' to share before
family and friends; vows which embodied 40 years of love
and commitment to each other and a desire to renew that
covenant of love for however long the Lord would give us

together, expressed in these words to each other:

> *Forty years ago when we joined our lives together we were certain we had something special. We hoped it would last and, by an act of faith, we made our promises. Upon that faith we began to build a life together. That commitment, as something special, has stayed with us and has been our source of strength. I promised to love you, to comfort you, to obey you and honour you; to forsake all others and to be faithful. These I have endeavoured to do and today I reconfirm those promises with all my heart.*

> *Through the years we have hurt and laughed; had life's ups and downs; and we have learned lessons that have shown us the meaning of true love. One of those lessons has been the difference between a love that lasts and one that gives up when the going gets tough.*

> *We have encouraged each other's dreams and forgiven each other's faults. We have faced problems and storms together and discovered the strength to go on. We have often remembered the word given to us on our Wedding Day that said, 'we would go through storms, but as long as we walked in the centre of God's will for us, the storms would not touch us'. This has been very real, especially when we both faced the storm of cancer.*

> *I promised it would be for better or for worse; for richer or for poorer; in sickness and in health; to love, cherish and obey, until death parted us. This is still my solemn vow.*

> *The rings on our fingers remind us of the commitment we made 40 years ago. They are the signs of our love and faithfulness. They remind me of my vow and covenant to you. Still today with my body I honour you; all that I am is your's; all that I have I share with you.*

*It has been a labour of love and we have become as
one, fighting against the odds and creating a
marriage that has lasted. My faith is still that we
have that something special that will make our
marriage last. Thank you for 40 wonderful years!
Our love has grown through the rough time and the
smooth times.*

*I thank you for your loyalty and faithfulness;
a commitment that has been total
and a real covenant.*

*When I said "I will", I promised to love, comfort,
honour and protect you; to forsake all other and to be
faithful to you. I meant it with all my heart. It has
lasted 40 years, and now I want to say it again to
you for all the years God gives us together.*

It was a very precious moment as we renewed our
commitment to each other in this way, before cutting our
Celebration Cake! The Lord knows the days He has
allotted to us and how I praise Him that He gave the
opportunity and provision for us to celebrate together. It
was like another Wedding Day!

Among Heather's cherished notes recorded in her
journals was that of 'An ancient Marriage Prayer' which
reads:

*May we two live our lives so happily together that God
may enjoy our union of heart and spirit with each other*

When God created Adam and Eve we read that, in that
initial unspoilt relationship, 'They heard the sound of the
Lord God as He was walking in the Garden.' (Genesis 3:10)
Man and wife were used to being in God's presence
together. It was a tangible pleasure to them. So it was for
Heather and I. We cherished our unity with Him and each

other. Those times when we read His Word together, when we worshipped Him together, and when with one heart and mind we prayed together. I so miss those times. They were precious.

Spoken of in the context of the 'benefits of wisdom', we read in Proverbs 3, verse 3 of *love and faithfulness* being two elements which are essential for a healthy life, and I believe a good marriage too! *Bind them around your neck*, we read, which suggests a halter or yoke, illustrating something that keeps us united and in step with our partner. *Write them too on the tablet of your heart* enabling them to go far deeper than just words or actions, and to be rooted in the very depths of our being. Heather saw these two elements as essential in our marriage. Therefore, she allowed the Lord to till the soil of her heart and to cultivate these godly fruits in her life. She truly was a wife of noble character, worth far more than rubies!

God-given life to enjoy

Heather believed that fun is something we create for ourselves, not something that life hands us! How true this is. She loved planning surprises for us to do together or with our family and friends and she was brilliant at keeping secrets! I treasure the memory of those fun times together. One such time was the occasion of my birthday. My diary indicated that I had a 'ministry' engagement that evening, but Heather had actually arranged a surprise 'Barn Dance Party' for me. I had not the slightest clue about any of her secret planning so it was a wonderful surprise, and such fun. I guess it was a 'ministry' evening really, but one with a difference!

Heather and I loved life, and we loved life together, enjoying each other's company. We saw enjoyment as an atmosphere we created simply by being together and seeking to bless each other. Our shared love for the county of Cornwall enabled us to simply take full advantage of our local area. I say 'simply' because one of our greatest loves was to take frequent drives to Fowey where we could look up the estuary and marvel at its beauty together.

When we had our lovely 'goldies' — *Honey* then *Petro* — we enjoyed our walks with them and they, along with us, probably thought 'what a wonderful area to live!' The sea and rivers to swim in, the beaches to play on, the woods to explore, the endless new people to meet in our home all seemed to make up for the holidays they had to have away from us at the kennels during Camp weeks!

In the midst of a busy schedule we saw time to relax as being very important, and often the vehicle for His provision too! For in green pastures we found His rest, and by still waters He restored our souls. What a wonderful Shepherd, who promised to supply everything we will ever need, with nothing lacking!

We loved to drive to the Moors for a relaxing time. Dartmoor was another favourite area, so much so that we actually spent a Christmas there together. In fact we had planned, and even booked, to do that again, but we had to cancel it at the last minute when Heather became so ill, just before her promotion to Glory.

Perhaps one of our favourite areas in the UK was the Lake District, where we spent some great holidays together. Many of you will know just how much Heather loved discovering history through our travels and one of her delights was when I was able to book a special holiday on the 'Royal Scotsman' about five years ago. Heather absolutely loved the scenery and we had a fantastic trip. One of the highlights was a visit to a Castle where we had afternoon tea with the Queen's representative! Another of the highlights was the conversations we had with our 'host' who ate with us on the train. There were around 30 of us as 'guests' on this particular holiday and one day he asked me the question "What do you do?" Apparently he had been watching us over the days. When we told him what we did he said, "The moment you two came on the train I knew there was something different about you." He then opened up to us and told us that his brother was a vicar, but he himself was a backslider. Heather was so excited by this conversation and by the fact that, without saying anything, he had noticed something different in us or rather, 'Someone' different! It was indeed a God-appointment and I trust that this was the start of his prodigal journey home.

The whole experience of travelling on the Royal Scotsman brought Heather so much pleasure—and me too as I saw what a blessing this was to her. I remain so grateful to Father that I was able to give expression to Heather in this way of how much I cherished and appreciated her as a brilliant wife and mother.

Dreams fulfilled

Madeira too was another of our favourite places, and one which we did plan to re-visit but had to cancel. Norway was another special place that Father allowed us to visit. But our greatest (and longest!) holiday ever was spending three weeks in South Africa in October 2005. It had been the dream of our hearts for about 30 years. In fact, during every Married Couples' Seminar which we conducted when we asked them to write a letter to their spouse—despite being the 'teachers'—we always wrote to each other too! And guess what we wrote when we came to the question 'What vision do you have that you haven't yet fulfilled?' Yes, it was our special holiday in Africa! How I thank God that He did grant us that wonderful experience together and allowed our dream to become reality, before Heather went to be with the Lord. His provision and timing was amazing and what a thrill it was to both of us.

A highlight of that time was that, although we had seen most of the 'big five' animals over our years of visiting Africa, we had never actually seen the leopard. We longed to just catch a glimpse of one and went out every morning and evening just hoping! But no, so we asked the Lord 'please help us to see one whilst we are here.' Just a few minutes after we had started out on our evening trip, which was the last of the 4 days, guess what we saw? A leopard *and* two cubs, and we were able to track them for a whole hour! What an amazing experience this was for both of us.

Heather loved seeing these splendid animals in the wild and over the years had delighted in every sighting of lions and their cubs, but during our safari trip together we also caught sight of lions mating. A recent TV nature documentary confirmed that this is a rarity to the public eye and cameramen often spend long hours, sometimes hundreds of hours, in seeking to track and film them. We spent a wonderful 4 days enjoying to the full the reality of 'our dream' and often exchanged memories of our safari experience together. Isn't it just so great to know that the things that matter to us matter to our Heavenly Father too, and He delights in giving us the desires of our hearts and 'the icing on the cake' too, so to speak!

Sharing from the 'store-house' of her heart...

Heather had a great love for Africa and the people loved her too. You should have seen all the mail that came in when news reached them that she had died. Messages which conveyed testimonies, tributes and such appreciation. Affectionately known as 'Mamma Heather', they held Heather in great honour and always looked forward to our visits and to all that she imparted from the 'storehouse' of her heart, both through her teaching of the Word of God, and through her real love for them. I guess she will always be remembered as 'Mamma Heather' as the rich legacy of her life and teaching continues to be passed on from one generation to another.

It was, of course, impossible for them to travel to England in order to give thanks to God with us for Heather's life, so instead they had their own times of remembrance and thanksgiving in their homeland, with those who had been so much part of our life and ministry over the years. Similar 'thanksgiving times' happened in other places around the world too. This spoke so much to me in my own loss for I knew it was not only me who had had to say 'goodbye' to a wife, but they too had lost a precious friend and teacher, one who they wanted to remember before God with 'thanksgiving'. No doubt also to join in the 'welcome home' celebrations of Heaven and to add their loud 'Amen's' to Father's 'Well done, good and faithful servant!'

We travelled lots together around the world as we ministered in various countries. In fact, our ministry took us to around 50 different nations and islands. What a privilege it was to share many of those times with Heather and to see for myself something of how God used her giftings to help others through her friendships, preaching, teaching, training and writing. She taught on such a wide range of subjects, through the revelation God gave as she studied His Word.

Much of our ministry, particularly in recent years, was to leaders and their wives, and in conducting Marriage Seminars. I guess we were given the privilege of helping hundreds of couples around the world, especially in Africa, where we found such a hunger for life-application Bible teaching. What a joy and encouragement it was for us to see God doing what only He can do as lives and marriages were transformed. To Him be all the glory!

Heather had a great love for history, especially Old Testament history, and she was given such clear insight and revelation into God's plans and purposes for His chosen land and people of Israel, which so many have said helped to bring the Word of God alive as they listened to her teaching. We were privileged to lead many tours to Israel in our years together and it was always fascinating to watch Heather just drinking in every new aspect of revelation or understanding as we were guided around that special land. Her journals are full of the weaving together of notes made during those tours and her study of the Scriptures. The richness of the legacy which Heather has left will, I am sure, continue to resource future generations.

Of course, this is also true of our ministry together here in this nation as Heather simply sought to give away all that God had imputed to her. Whether that was speaking to crowds from a platform, leading small groups, on a one-to-one level with someone who needed personal help and wisdom or in just supporting me in a very practical way, Heather was no different, for her heart was to minister to the individual, even when facing the crowds. How like Jesus her Saviour who, even when addressing the multitude, saw the individual heart and their need, and reached out to them with compassion!

She opens her hand to the poor, yes,she reaches out her filled hands to the needy . . . (Proverbs 31:20 AMP) this was Heather's heart. She was one of the most generous people I have ever known. In fact, sometimes if I didn't watch out there would not be enough to pay the electric bill! She only really knew how to give and she gave, and gave and gave! But through it all she taught me so many lessons. When big bills came in I would often say, "Oh dear!" But not Heather. She would soon challenge me by saying, "Come on. Trust Him. He has never let us down yet." And she was right!

When God gave us our first home the enemy tried his hardest to make us doubt God's promises by saying, "You'll never be able to pay the rates." Had we made a wrong move or had we heard God? We were sure it was the latter, and especially so when we were in a conference and someone read the Scripture where Jesus tells Peter to go and catch a fish and inside its mouth would be a coin to use to go and pay his taxes. Amazingly, the translation which was read said, '**rates** and taxes'. Through this God spoke to us very clearly telling us not to worry about the rates for He **would** supply. And miraculously after the meeting a man came up to us and told us that every rate bill we received, we were to send to him! Again God kept His promise, and through this man **every** rate bill was paid for our first house.

Secure in the knowledge of God's faithfulness to His Word, Heather never held back in the face of need, but gave out of the overflow of her heart, trusting that God would honour His promises and supply all our needs as we sowed first I into His Kingdom and He did! In fact many things that we are involved in today, like 'Hope for the Handicapped in Tanzania', were very close to Heather's heart.

Making disciples of all nations

One of the areas of rich blessing we shared together over our years in ministry is that of seeing the 'Evangelism Training Course' birthed, first in this nation, then moving in more recent years to the continent of Africa. Heather has been a vital part of this training programme as students of all ages have come from many parts of the world to be trained in response to the great commission of Jesus to his disciples, recorded in Matthew 28: 19, *"Therefore go and make disciples of all nations, baptizing them in the Name of the Father and of the Son and of the Holy Spirit."* Verse 20, from The Message, concludes: *"Then instruct them in the practice of all I have commanded you. I'll be with you as you do this, day after day after day, right up to the end of the age."*

Heather had the joy of seeing many of those students go out to serve the Lord and bear rich fruit; and what a joy it was to her heart. With that 'baton' now handed on to others, we honour her for every way she has inspired others to 'go' in Christ's Name to seek the lost. I am sure those students will never forget the passion and challenge of Heather's words of encouragement, " course you can!" And they will ever ring in the heart of those who continue on Team too. They certainly will in mine!

Our annual *Good News Crusade* Easter Conventions were pioneered in Ipswich, Suffolk in 1959. Heather, too, became involved in these after the first two years, and we then worked on them together for the next 19 years, after which they moved on to other venues as they developed. One of the venues was Canvey Island in Essex where Dr. Derek Prince was one of our main speakers. Along with Dr. Judson Cornwall, who was a great friend to us both, they both ministered with us on many occasions at the various locations for our conventions, camps and conferences and became much-loved speakers.

These events led on to the establishing of the Deeper Life Conferences and Family Camps in the early days of our ministry through *Good News Crusade*, and what an impact these times together have had on countless individuals and families over the years. Launching out in planning those first camps was a huge step of faith. *Who would come? What would it cost to organize? And what would it involve for everyone to be together for a whole week!* Very soon those questions began to be answered. People came, not just once but year-on-year, and they brought others, who in turn brought others! We knew we had tapped into something which was on Father's heart for us to provide and, although there have been changes in the times, places and structure of those weeks together, the vision has not changed and for many Camp weeks still remain one of the highlights of their year.

Our very first GNC venture was at Lytchett Minster at Post Green which came about through the way God spoke specifically to us through Jean Darnell. She was at an event at Post Green as a 'day speaker' and to our surprise she brought a prophetic word that there was someone in the meeting who had a large meeting tent which the Lord wanted to use. You can imagine how we felt, especially when some people who were aware that we had a tent turned and pointed to us! Seeing this, Jean then addressed us personally and said we would be back at Post Green in August. Even more of a surprise, as it was already late April/May at the time! But we had a real sense that God had called us to be there and that is how our camps started. A big new step of faith into unchartered waters! Little did we ever dream at the time just what Father was going to unfold as he launched us out into a wider and deeper ministry. No wonder GNC has gained the reputation of 'deep-end ministry' over the years that have followed!

Many will remember the early Family Camps and Deeper Life Conferences at Blaithwaite in Cumbria, not just because of the mud but because of the rich ministry and personal encounters with the Lord they had during those weeks. Others will remember the Deeper Life Camps at Newbury, Berkshire. Chadacre Agricultural College, near Bury St. Edmunds in Suffolk became an additional venue for our Family Camps from 1977 and this became 'home' for these special camp weeks together for many years before moving on to Brooksby Hall Agricultural College, Leicester. When, in 1980, we moved to having two annual Family Camps, we continued our camps at Chadacre, moving from Blaithwaite to The Three Counties Showground at the foot of the Malvern Hills in Worcestershire as the second venue—and a meeting place with God. This change gave us quite a central site, again in a lovely area, where we saw the numbers of people of all ages attending gradually increase from hundreds into a few thousand during the years of 1980 to 1990. Other venues have, of course, been Brackenhurst College near

Nottingham in 1991, followed by Lackham College, near Chippenham, Wiltshire and in more recent years Taunton, Somerset. Although there have been many changes since camps started (not least in Heather and I starting to hand over the main leadership and planning of Camps to our son Stephen and his wife Anne two years ago), the annual Family Camps continue to be special encounter weeks with God for children, young people and adults—and lots of fun too!

As Heather and I celebrated 21 years of full-time ministry together at our Chadacre Family Camp, Heather particularly wanted Dr. Judson Cornwall to share that occasion with us as guest speaker. We had a great time of celebration and thanksgiving to God for His faithfulness over the years. Many other friends and GNC supporters shared in that time with us, too, which was ably presented by TV actor Timmy Bateson. As well as appreciating Dr. Cornwall's deep knowledge and clear teaching of the Word of God, Heather considered him to be a real gentleman and father-figure in the Body of Christ. He was always willing to fly over from the USA to be with us at *Good News Crusade* and we enjoyed many occasions of ministry together. As a Bible teacher himself, he was particularly blessed by Heather's ministry and teaching.

Although many other Christian camps have sprung up over the years (and we pray God's richest blessings on them too) people do say that there is something uniquely special about GNC Family Camps. It was very much a pioneering venture for us initially, and we certainly never set out to be different for difference sake, but in keeping to the 'blue print' that the Lord gave us I guess they do remain unique. It blesses us to now to be hosting the grand-children of those who first came to our early camps; an aspect of camps which is very 'family'. These weeks together were something that held a very special place in Heather's heart and her motherly input, into both adult's and young people's lives, was always so much appreciated.

Creativity that knew no bounds!

The Message says of the virtuous wife, spoken of in Proverbs 31, that *She's up before dawn, preparing breakfast for her family and organizing her day.* (Proverbs 31:15 MSG) This so clearly describes Heather, and because she was an organizer her whole life reflected this in the way she planned and prepared and in her expectations of others too! Eugene Peterson goes on to say of such a wife, *First thing in the morning, she dresses for work, rolls up her sleeves, eager to get started. She senses the worth of her work, is in no hurry to call it quits for the day.* (Proverbs 31:18 MSG) Heather truly set about all she did vigorously, and younger people found it quite hard to keep up with her! Not because she was always racing through life as if on a hundred meter dash, but because of her achievements in all she set her heart to do.

Breakfast time in our home was, as much as possible, seen as a time when we could be together at the start of a new day. Heather always sought to be well prepared for those times with either the provision of food to partake of together, or at least food for thought and prayer when there was a lack in those early days of mission trips abroad! For there were times when the necessary food supplies for the family were the miraculous answer to prayers. Heather taught them well to trust their Heavenly Father's promises and to call on Him and He never failed them. They never went hungry and they certainly learnt the importance of the prayer the Lord gave to all of us: *"Give us today our daily bread"* (Matthew 6:11) and of their own dependence on Him. Truly a wife and a mother whose teaching began in the home.

One of Heather's great loves was cooking and she was always keen to glean recipes from the various countries where we ministered, or to search out others which were creative and appetizing. If she could not find them she just created her own and was brilliant in producing some outstanding dishes. There were a number of favourites which we enjoyed back home. I think particularly of one from Chile of a pumpkin with the seeds removed, which was then stuffed with corn on the cob, steak, peaches and various fruits. Such a tasty savoury and sweet dish that gets my taste buds going when I think about it! Being one who enjoys my food, I so appreciated a wife with such amazing culinary skills, and one whose heart was always keen to extend the provisions on our table to many others over the years, through the gift of hospitality. The delights of Heather's food remain a talking point for many who shared time in our home. Despite my efforts I haven't risen to those heights of fame yet—but I am trying!

This Christmas, my first and only one without Heather for 43 years, I knew I would be facing many changes, but I guess I was not prepared for a special surprise. Every year since we were married Heather had always made the Danish Christmas dish 'Rice a la man', and it has been so much part of our 'traditional' English Christmas. No-one else in the family knew how to make it, and we had no recipe—and no Heather—so I was adjusting myself to the fact that this would no longer be part of my festive diet! However, Father had this all planned and about 4 o'clock on Christmas Eve the doorbell rang. No it wasn't David Abbott who loved to bring his bowl to the table for this annual festive delicacy! But there stood Yetta (a Danish friend, who was one of Heather's bridesmaids) with a bowl of 'Rice a la man' in her hands—for me! Needless to say I just dissolved into tears at the goodness of our tender and ever-loving Heavenly Father who cares about the smallest details in our lives and provides friends that care enough to be the channel of His provision too.

Time—a gift from God

Heather valued life and she valued time, seeking never to waste any of it! Many people speak of 'spending time' but Heather's attitude was that of 'redeeming' or 'buying up' time because she realized that it was a gift from God, a gift that is so easily stolen from us through idleness. Therefore, any potential idle moments (even whilst travelling or waiting at airports) were seen as opportunities to be creative in some way, whether that be in writing, knitting, sewing, embroidery or some other creative craft, in planning some new project in the home, or even in dreaming and developing some fresh creative aspect of our ministry together. In fact she was an expert in multi-tasking and seemed to be able to put her hands to almost anything and make a success of it—with photography and knowing how to repair a car being amongst her list of achievements! Two of the most treasured pieces of furniture which grace our home are a Victorian Nursing Chair and a Victorian Rocking Chair, both of which Heather completely renovated herself, and many have said that she did an expert job on them. These are real highlights of her creative work, and all around our home are tapestries and other kinds of needlecraft which constantly remind me of God's gift of an extremely expressive and gifted wife.

Perhaps one the things which I will treasure most is a knitted cardigan; the last thing Heather made for me before she died. She started and completed it in those final months and weeks when she was becoming increasingly weak and so unwell. It represents a gift to me that is much more than just a cardigan, for right to the end she gave of herself so lovingly as she sought to serve and bless me.

A friend of many years, recalls the time when I arrived back from one of my early trips to Africa with 'heaps' of brightly coloured and patterned material, all about the size of table cloths. I guess I thought that such a gift would really bless Heather! And it did, for with her skilled eye for design she set about cutting them up and making them into 'African' shirts for me and some of the other team members. Heather loved making clothes for herself and the family and always loved seeking out different fabrics to bring home from our overseas trips. Perhaps I started something when I brought her that first bundle of African fabric!

Seeing the bigger picture

Over the years travelling became a huge part of our life and God used this in a number of ways, not least in the bigger picture of the world which it brought to us and the awareness of the many people groups who had never had the opportunity of hearing the Gospel. For that reason Heather loved travel, whether it was around the world or across our own nation, because we were responding to His call to take the message of His wonderful salvation wherever He opened doors to us.

Eugene Peterson's interpretation of Proverbs 31: 6 speaks of the business acumen imparted to the virtuous wife. This is something which I saw so clearly in Heather as she loved to seek out and plan economic deals for our travels, and how best we could make good use of our time and resources. I am sure that her godly wisdom enabled us to achieve much more than would have otherwise been the case.

Our travels in this country involved a lot of driving and again Heather was such a support to me in that. Often I would be scheduled to speak soon after our arrival, so Heather would take the wheel and allow me to just rest from that responsibility. On the occasions when I drove she was always a brilliant navigator. Whichever way we handled our journeys, her sensitivity and thoughtfulness meant so much and always gave expression of her loving support and thoughtfulness.

I have already mentioned the way that God called us into marriage and service together and the way our ministry began and developed. The unfolding of this has been an exciting adventure for us both, and so often along that path new inspiration has been given to Heather as to how best we could up-date our communication skills in an increasingly technological world. It was Heather, therefore, who took the initiative to teach herself how to use 'PowerPoint' so that together we could keep 'with it' in our presentations. I am so grateful for a wife who saw the importance of this and who has left me with a knowledge of the basic skills of how to continue those presentations; with a little bit of help and encouragement from my grandsons!

Ingrid Trobish said, "A woman who is constantly learning new things and who is skilled in at least one will be both confident and competent." Both those aspects were increasingly reflected in Heather's life, because she was one who was always seeking to expand her knowledge and understanding. She loved books and was an avid reader. In fact more often than not she was found with a Bible or a book propped up in front of her to read, whilst she was undertaking a craft creation with her hands! Perhaps that is why the work she produced was so stunning. I can recall many a cross-stitch bookmark being lovingly created in Heather's hands whilst she was meditating on particular Scriptures, and of how these crafted words proved to be so prophetic when Heather gave them to those she had been praying for.

Embracing change

Over the years as we journeyed in God together we were aware of Him confirming our call and 'enlarging the place of our tent, stretching out our tent curtains, lengthening our cords and strengthening our stakes' (Isaiah 54:2) often in ways that were beyond our wildest dreams and human capabilities. Those times were very humbling as we knew we were out of our depth without Him! Whatever challenge Heather was presented with, if she knew it was an opportunity to become more God-dependent, she would face it knowing that He would always bring the enabling somehow, whether that was through study, research, training or, more especially, directly through His supernatural power. Hence her affirmation "Course you can." Heather knew that, just as NO thing is impossible to God, so is doing nothing, for God is never passive. He is always at work making the impossible possible! So she trusted Him totally when He was stretching her beyond her human limits, knowing that His grace and enabling would not fail. In more recent years it was such a joy for me to see Heather released more fully into the areas of ministry God had clearly anointed her for, and to see that anointing increase as she stepped forward into change.

A highlighted entry in one of Heather's journals, which obviously meant a lot to her, was **"The will of God will never lead you where the grace of God cannot keep you."** Of course, Heather knew this to be true too at all times, even when God was bringing change in other ways. Change which meant stepping back from some areas of ministry or responsibility in order to be strengthened and equipped to move forward into something new, or even to give space for others to serve. Over the years a number of such prophetic words were given to us through a number of trusted Church leaders both here in our own nation and around the world, and, as these words were confirmed, it sometimes meant big changes. These changes were not always easy to embrace, but Heather especially knew that they would be for our good and God's greater glory so she was always there to encourage me if I was hesitant, and to raise my vision for what God wanted to unfold and lead us into. How grateful I am that He gave me a wife who did not allow me to get stuck in familiar ruts, when there was change to be embraced.

In sickness and in health

Heather's love of books led her to become an author in her own right and many of her books have been best sellers over the years. We also co-authored a number of other books, our most recent one being *God on the Mountain is still God in the Valley* which tells the story of our journey when we faced cancer within 15 months of each other back in 2000 and 2001. Facing that path herself, before I was totally through with my own cancer journey, was something we had not expected, but I honour her for the courage and bravery she showed as she faced that time with a sure confidence in God. During that time we were both so blessed and uplifted by watching the Gaither series of DVDs—the chorus of one of the songs being:

> *For the God on the mountains is still God in the*
> *valley,*
> *When things go wrong He'll make them right,*
> *And the God of the good times is still God in the bad*
> *times,*
> *The God of the day is still God in the night.*

And as these words rang out they so ministered to our spirits that we joined in singing them as an affirmation from our own hearts, knowing that He is not only there with us all the time but that He remains good!

Following Heather's surgery, when she came home I took on being her resident part-time 'nurse', a role which, along with other dear family and friends, she had fulfilled for me just a few months earlier. Knowing that she then had to face a course of chemotherapy over the next 18 weeks, followed by radiotherapy for 25 days was not an easy path to tread, but Heather kept hold of the hand of God as she stepped out on this additional part of the journey, trusting Him to keep her strong and positive. And He did! The predicted side-effects were kept to a minimum and only for a few brief hours did she suffer any form of depression or acute tiredness. In fact the medics even adjusted the timetable of Heather's treatment, with a shorter break than normal between finishing her chemotherapy and commencing her radiotherapy, which allowed her to take a small part in the 'Evangelism Training Course' and then to go on to be part of the national 'Ladies' Conference' as arranged over a year in advance. Heather's heart thrilled with excitement when she realized all the attention to detail on Father's 'Master timetable'!

Till death us do part

Having previously faced major surgery for gallstone removal, her courage and bravery did not end here as medically she had more to face when soon after this time she needed urgent surgery for a complicated hernia. Although all of these things left her physically weakened, she remained strong in spirit and so determined to *forget what was behind* [not focusing on it] . . . *and to press on to take hold of that for which Christ Jesus had taken hold of her,* (Philippians 3:13-14) always fixing her eyes on Him.

Prior to what was to be her last year at Camp in the summer of 2006, Heather had still been feeling somewhat weak and unwell but she did not let this deter her preparations in bringing the messages she knew God had laid on her heart for the Camp. Many were touched by our son Stephen as he invited her forward to speak saying 'it's a great privilege for me to invite my mother to the platform to bring us God's Word' — a somewhat ordinary invitation he had given many times before, and yet there seemed to be something so poignant about this occasion. None of us could ever have imagined, though, that these would be the last messages she would actually ever deliver when she stood before us in that marquee at Taunton, for she stood before us all in His obvious strength and anointing. I was so proud of her.

The following week Heather's health really deteriorated and she had to be admitted to hospital for tests and treatment, and this became the pattern over the next few weeks and months. Another course of chemotherapy had to be faced as new diagnoses were made, all of which brought increasing weakness. Together we sought to remain positive, praying, believing, trusting God. Some days that was easier than others, but deep down we never doubted the Sovereignty of God even when our humanity gave way to doubts and fears. The medics and subsequent Hospice staff were wonderful in all their administration of treatment and care, but we could see that Heather was becoming physically weaker and her body was deteriorating as pints of fluid were being drained away from her lungs and she underwent a pleurodesis. Despite our faith and fervent prayers it became more and more obvious that her time to go home to Father was drawing nearer, and her journals, which she kept even up to that point, record some very precious moments of intimate preparation for Heaven.

During those final few months from late August 2006 to 13th March 2007, along with our family, we shared much together, including having to say a tearful goodbye to our lovely Golden Retriever, *Petro*. That was a painful parting for both of us, especially as he had been such a faithful friend over the years, even through the company he brought Heather in her room at the Hospice during his visits. Dogs have such a wonderful way of sensing what is most needed when their loved ones are ill, don't they, and *Petro* certainly did. Heather looked forward to his visits to her, so the parting of this very faithful friend was another big change to face.

We went on to shed many more tears, and times of

laughter too, as we recalled and appreciated the many experiences we had been able to share together during our 43 years of marriage. We reflected on all the rich experiences we had enjoyed with our family, and the blessings of our grand-children, who are all so special. We thought of friends, we read God's Word, we prayed, we worshipped and somehow all those things became so much more precious to us as Heather was journeying home.

As I left Heather's hospice room at 7.00 p.m. on the 13th March 2007 to take a little break back home I took hold of her hand and said "Haven't we had 43 wonderful years to be together?" As she looked into my eyes, and probably the horizons of Heaven's courts too, she quietly, yet confidently said, "Yes, and we'll have a lot more."

Just two short hours following that precious moment, during which our son Joel spent his own time with his Mum, I had an unexpected text from Heather herself calling me to 'come quick'. I sensed the urgency and returned immediately to take hold of her hand for a few fleeting moments as Father reached out to her and led her into His eternal home.

Heather was a very beautiful wife in every way who always sought to clothe herself in a way that was honouring to the Lord, and as a wife and mother. It was a principle she both taught and lived. She loved colour and her flare in the use of colours just seemed to enhance her personality in a way which never took away her uniqueness as 'Heather', but instead reflected His beauty from within her. That inner radiance of *unfading beauty of a woman who feared the Lord* drew people to her like a magnet, but she knew how to channel that seeking to her Saviour within! Only eternity will fully reveal those whose lives have been transformed by the Calvary love of a

Saviour as Heather reached out to them through a life laid
down on His altar of obedience. But this I do know, she is
certainly enjoying worshipping with some of them already!

When the Lord calls me home I know I will join her too,
and together we will enjoy eternity forever. But until that
day I remain so thankful to the Lord for the gift of such a
wonderful wife in Heather, one worth far more than
precious gems, who belonged to Him long before He
entrusted her to me.

Heather was one who kept a personal journal of her
own day by day walk with the Lord over the years, right
up to the time when she went to be with Him in March
2007, and it has been very precious to me to read through
Heather's notes in those journals which she left. Obviously
I saw all these notes as very personal to Heather, so it was
not until she died that I looked into her journals. I want to
close this chapter about my devoted wife by sharing with
you what Heather wrote:

> *Having to face the reality that I may only have a few*
> *weeks or months at the most left to live, I feel no*
> *regrets—only disappointment at the times I failed and*
> *got angry! I feel my life has been full of God's blessing.*
> *I have had a wonderful husband—the very best God*
> *could have given me. My family have surpassed my*
> *expectations. I am so very proud of all their*
> *accomplishments, especially Nigel and Faith who both*
> *had struggles academically while at school.*
>
> *I feel disappointment that I will leave Don as I have*
> *felt one of God's calls on my life was to care for Him.*
> *God called me to be a 'help' and I felt the main thrust*
> *of this was for Don. Now it would appear that I am*
> *not to fulfil this to the full. Another disappointment is*
> *that I will not see the grand-children grow and*

accomplish the things I know God has spoken to me will be fulfilled in their lives. One thing I know — God said there will never cease to be at least one in each generation of our family that will serve Him! I was looking forward to seeing which grandchild had the calling of God to full-time ministry, because I felt that was what He meant.

I am at peace and can say that I feel total joy and peace in me. No fear of death — it is just a shadow. I am trusting God to fulfil His purpose in my life. If that has been accomplished then 'so be it'. If not then I look forward to God working a miracle and astounding us and the medical profession. It is God's will that I look to. His purpose for my life MUST be accomplished. I have been trying to write 'My Story' and hope someone will be able to take it on and finish it for me, as I feel that this is one thing God has asked me to do.

I have enjoyed my life serving God in the way we have. I have enjoyed my family — each and every one of them. I took Nigel and Julia as my own. I felt God gave them to me, and I tried my best to be all that I could to them. I never once felt them a burden or any other negative thing. I can only trust I fulfilled what God wanted me to with them.

My trust is still in God to bring me through, whatever that means and whichever way it goes. God is Lord and Sovereign.

Heather
10th February 2007

- 4 -

An Amazing Mother and Homemaker

These are the commands, decrees and laws the LORD your God directed me to teach you to observe . . . So that you, your children and their children after them may fear the LORD your God.

Love the LORD your God with all your heart and with all your soul and with all your strength. These commandments which I give you today are to be upon your hearts. Impress them on your children. Talk about them when you sit at home and when you walk along the road, when you lie down and when you get up. Tie them as symbols on your hands and bind them on your foreheads. Write them on the doorframes of your houses and on your gates.

Deuteronomy 6: 1-9 (selected)

In our ministry together, particularly in more recent years, Heather and I were increasingly involved in teaching on 'Family Life' and 'Parenting' in Churches and groups around the world, and one of the things which

Heather emphasized a lot to Christian parents was that 'You are the first example to your children of what a Christian is.' And how true this is. Apparently Abraham Lincoln was once asked "What is the greatest book you have ever read?" His succinct reply was **"My mother!"** Probably not the answer expected, but nevertheless one which spoke volumes about how he saw his mother. And, asked the same question, I could well imagine our children and those who have been part of our 'extended family' thinking the same way about Heather, for her very life was like an open book.

I am a great believer in the importance of following **the** Maker's instructions, as you will know (hence my book title on the subject) and the first thing a parent is told to do in Scripture is to teach (their) children the Word of God. I believe that this also means teaching them *how to hear His word* and *how to apply its Truth in their lives.* Its great to live in a country where good Bible-believing Churches can still do this openly, as well as some of our schools, but we need to see that God gave this responsibility firstly to parents in the home. It is here where that teaching first needs to be 'worked in' and 'lived out' with clear integrity. It is a Scriptural principle that what we do as parents is picked up by our family; and conversely so if it is in conflict with what we say!

Clearing the 'land mines'!

As a family we have always sought to be very real with each other about how we are feeling and often very direct with our words. Sometimes life could be a very moving experience from one to another, as our family can testify! As Heather describes in her book *Ouch! That Hurt,* often our behaviour and actions come out of situations or through relating to people: family members, school teachers, leaders, friends. Being hurt, let down or betrayed by people whom we trust, or criticised unjustly by others, leaves us very vulnerable if these hurts are not dealt with. It is so easy to try to push the effects of these encounters under the surface, but the trouble is if they are still alive, they live on like 'land mines' which are triggered when others tread on them, causing yet more hurt and injury.

For this reason, I want to share something right at the start of this chapter which the family, or even friends, would probably not feel right about recounting, but which was, nevertheless, part of our life together and a transforming part of Heather's walk with the Lord. It was the time, many years ago, when she received ministry to be freed from rejection and how it had affected her life. The freedom and change that this brought was so evident and life-changing in our home and family, that I share it as a testimony to the way Heather sought the Lord for His answers, when she knew in her inner self that things weren't right.

When Heather was at her senior school, the Girls' Grammar School, she was reprimanded and disciplined for walking with her brother through the local park (which she had to do in order to catch the bus home), while she was in her school uniform. Her brother, who went to the Boys' Grammar School, was also in his school uniform. According to school rules, this was something that was not seen as 'correct' so she was taken before the Head Mistress; the one and only time that this happened in her whole school life. She was also taken before the local vicar, who was one of the school governors. Heather felt this procedure was very unjust and she became hurt by being unnecessarily blamed for something quite normal and innocent.

Because of this incident, when someone (even the family or myself) wanted to talk with Heather about anything, her reaction would be that she was being blamed and she would feel rejected. This would happen even if we were coming in harmony and agreement to talk through an issue: she would end up feeling rejected and taking on unnecessary blame. At times it was something we had to work through together and it did affect the atmosphere of the home (and our relationship with others), because under the surface was rage which found release somehow.

Although Heather was not one to make excuses, she had come to accept it was part of her and that she, and others, needed to learn to live with it. That is, until the Lord put his finger on the root problem! Yes, Heather had prayed; she had sought the Lord for self-control, and even asked others to pray for her, but the deep inner rage was still there. It only took a new situation to arise and there would be a sudden eruption and none of us ever knew quite what would 'trigger' it, or when, because she would so often blame others for rejecting her, when that was clearly not the case.

Perhaps this is striking a cord with some of you who are reading this, so let me get to the key which opened Heather's 'prison' and brought her such freedom and transformation. It was the moment she was released from rejection and that inner rage had gone. The root had been dealt with, because Heather had gone to the only One who can heal our hurts, deliver us from bondage and set us free from the power of sin in our lives—**the Lord Jesus Christ.** Heather loved to teach on 'The Power of the Cross' and we certainly saw the evidence of Jesus' conquering power released in her life. It was a wonderfully real experience for Heather and she rejoiced even more when I used to say to many of our friends, "Its like living with a new wife." It was, and no doubt our children thought they had a new mother too!

Another time was at one of our Summer Family Camps, when a visiting speaker brought Heather a word about 'grieving'. At first she could not relate to this, because she felt it must refer to the loss of a loved one through death, but some eighteen months later the Lord showed her that the grief she was carrying related to broken relationships. Although she was still doing all the 'right' things in terms of prayer, Bible reading and even ministering, she knew deep down that it had affected her own personal relationship with the Lord and with us as a family too. Heather realized she was becoming hard and defensive, because she was unsure of letting anyone get close to her again and of taking the risk of being hurt again. It was such a natural reaction, but she knew she had allowed the enemy a foothold in her life which was affecting her and she needed to do something about it in order to be free again. She recounts, "That morning God showed me how Jesus had dealt with grief in my place on the Cross. I no longer had to carry that burden of grief." What new freedom Heather knew when she could lay her burden down at the Cross and exchange it for the freedom that Jesus brought for us at Calvary.

There were many other times, too, when Heather realized that she had allowed other issues, such as criticism, to bring blockages in her life, but she was always one to bring those things before the Lord and seek His forgiveness and release. Our life and ministry together continually brought us into the public arena where people were facing real life situations and looking for answers to their personal problems. Therefore, Heather and I knew that we needed to be real and honest about those 'Calvary times' in our lives, if we were going to be transparent and honest, as people seeking to help others find a deeper walk with the Lord—especially with our own family, who see us as we really are!

Teaching begins in the home

One of the earliest and clearest examples of home teaching we see in Scripture is that of the boy Samuel, born to Elkanah and Hannah, and dedicated to the Lord in fulfilment of Hannah's promised vow to Him in answer to the deep cries of her heart. As we too give thanks to the Lord for His gift to us through the birth of our children, so we also need to dedicate ourselves to Him as we seek to fulfil our role as godly parents—and especially so as we seek to take our responsibilities seriously and honour Him in today's society. It was in the home that Samuel was taught to hear the voice of God and where better for our children to learn that too. Talking to God and listening for His answers is shown by example as vital for our lives; reading His Word and seeking to obey Him is foundational; and sharing together helps and encourages us in life-application teaching.

Heather and I saw these principles as key in our parenting role, and in the life of our home and family, so establishing the 'Family Altar' was of real importance to us, so much so that whoever was sharing our home with us as we met together, and therefore formed part of our household, became a natural part of those times too. Perhaps in today's culture the 'Family Altar' would be seen as a bit 'old fashioned', but, whatever name we like to give such a place where we meet before God as a family or 'household' it is still vital if we are going to build family God's way. To have a time and a place where we model what is most important to us; a personal intimate relationship with the Living God that puts Him first in our lives. For if we really believe, as we do, that our children are a heritage from the Lord then we constantly need to be asking ourselves "What inheritance am I passing on to them that will keep that heritage alive?"

Each child a gift from God

As some of you will know from my own testimony and Heather's introduction to this book, the day that Heather became my wife she also dedicated herself to fulfil the role of mother to my two eldest children, Nigel (then 8) and Julia (then 5), who had previously affectionately been known to them as "Auntie Heather!" For a while Nigel and Julia continued to live with their grandparents in Suffolk, which had been 'home' to all of us following my marriage breakdown. In those early years of our marriage, whilst we kept good, open relationships with both the children and their grandparents, we lived apart from them except for regular visits and longer holiday times together at Easter, summer and Christmas, until the time came when they both wanted to move over to Cornwall and become a 'blended' part of our new family.

Up until then I perhaps had not fully realized what an effect my marriage breakdown had had on Nigel as a young boy, as at that time it was not such a common happening as sadly it is today. Nor had I realized his sense of shame at school by not being part of what his friends saw as a 'normal family' — feelings which perhaps caused him to seek peer approval in his early teens and to face hard times at school. So Nigel and Julia's decision to move to Cornwall filled us with delight when, at the age of 15 and 12 respectively, they moved in to join Heather and myself, and their new (half) brother Stephen who had just started school. A new chapter of life began for us all at that time. Nigel recalls that moment as being a natural step to take, yet one that was very special, even as he adjusted to leaving his grandparents and friends back in Suffolk and becoming part of our home and new family life in Cornwall.

> In the eulogy that Nigel wrote 'in honour of Heather — a special mother', he says.

> *"I was only a small boy when I first met someone who I initially called 'Auntie Heather'. This young lady soon became very special to me, for although she was but 11 years older, she helped fill the vast 'Mum-shaped' void that had appeared in my life years earlier. I can remember feeling so blessed and relieved*

*when I was first allowed to call her 'Mum', a while
before her marriage to Dad, a year or two after we first
met. After all she was such a young lady of only 17 or
18 years old! My grandparents had stood in the gap
and devoted around ten years of their lives in raising
my sister and I, but now I was to have someone I could
look to as a 'Mum' and I could start to feel 'normal'
again."*

In her teaching on 'blended families', Heather strongly
believed that *any child is a gift from God—no matter how that
child comes to be part of your family,* and so it was that Nigel
and Julia felt very loved and accepted as her 'family' right
from the start. Each individual in the family was seen as a
gift from God, and I cannot remember Heather ever
referring to either of them as 'step children' or treating
them as any different to the rest of her children. As far as
Heather was concerned, we were all one big family, so
much so that Stephen had no idea that Nigel and Julia were
his so-called 'half' brother and sister until he was in his
teens! Nigel and Julia were, of course, living with us all in
Cornwall when Joel and Faith were born, and although
their relationship with each other was naturally different as
true brother and sister, they all developed good family
relationships with each other and with Heather and I.

Proverbs 14:1 says *The wise woman builds her house, but
with her hands the foolish one tears hers down.'* Heather sought
to be a wise 'builder' of the family and home, believing it
is important it is to 'create' a home for the family to enjoy.
In her teaching she used to say, "God has made provision
for us, as mothers, to be to our children all that He needs us
to be to them. Our responsibility as mothers is to create the
atmosphere of 'home'. To make it a place that they will
want to return to because they will know 'home' is where
they are accepted, where they can just be themselves, and
where they are loved and cared for unconditionally."
Right from the start Heather sought to become a friend to

both Nigel and Julia, thus gaining their respect, before ever she tried to have any authority in their lives, and she always showed them great respect too. What wisdom—a principle which they obviously appreciated as they adapted to family life with us.

Nigel was becoming a grown-up working man when some of the family were still quite young, and, as I spent quite long periods ministering away from home during missions and preaching tours, he almost became a father figure in the home, with certain delegated disciplinary measures to administer to his younger siblings! No doubt this meant that he had to grow up early through taking on those responsibilities, but it did not hinder his relationships in the family and perhaps helped to develop the leadership skills that are so apparent now. Heather helped and encouraged Nigel a lot in his growing up years as she was the more 'home based' one with me away a lot.

Moving straight from school life in Suffolk to a working life as an apprentice printer in Cornwall, almost immediately, was a huge transition for him, but Heather was there to support him all the way. He had previously considered the thought of a career whilst he was still at school, possibly that of training as a PE teacher, but he became more and more drawn to the thought of leaving school and training in printing as he considered this would be both fulfilling and also be a help to us in our work and ministry. This gave us a window into Nigel's heart to really become a part of both our family and work. He comments, "Mum was feisty and forthright, but she was a bridge for me in that time, and was always there as a listener, encourager and helper. I respected her greatly as she became a real mother to me."

In 1974 Nigel met Barbara (who incidentally was saved as I preached the Gospel in a meeting she attended) and they married in 1976. Heather, along with me, was always accepting of Barbara, encouraging and supporting them all the way to walk in the centre of God's will for them. When this proved to be moving out to Tanzania as missionaries, with no visible means of support financially, Heather herself was so supportive and encouraged them to keep trusting God, the One who never fails to keep His promises. It meant a lot to them that they could trust Him through Heather undertaking to handle all their day-to-day administration back here in this country. These very practical things are a necessary part of our expression of love and encouragement to our children and Heather always saw the importance of this as a Mum who was committed to faith building.

In his tribute to Heather, Nigel highlighted three particular qualities that he recognized and appreciated in his 'Mum'.

"Firstly, she was very generous. She quickly made space for two small children to be part of her life, and keenly shared the rest of her life with us. She took us unreservedly as her own and we never had any reason to feel different. This unconditional love was such a great thing to give and something I had not had from anyone else. Some years ago when Julia and myself desired to find our own 'natural Mum'. Heather saw this as quite alright, realizing that it would probably be something we would desire to do one day. There was never any self-seeking and typically I received only encouragement from her. Secondly, she was mature. Not an ordinary teenager, even of her own 50's generation. Wise advice and counsel were her hallmarks and she was always the first to remind me of the debt of honour I owed to my sacrificial grandparents. Thirdly, she was committed. Mum was the prime example of a person devoted to Jesus Christ; serving Him, whatever the personal cost to herself, even through her last difficult months. Only hours before she died, not realizing the events of the evening to follow, Dad and I were discussing a day trip to London the following Saturday, which Mum was insisting he fulfilled!

"Whilst it would be true to say that Mum was quite strongly opinionated, she was well able to articulate her views without causing offence. She was also one who was able to speak her mind and then let things rest, and could handle criticism without personally taking offence. The key being that she was a very secure person in God, and also in whom she was in Him."

Heather saw her role as a mother and a homemaker as a vital one, believing that there is no contradiction in the Bible between a homemaker and a career. And there isn't. God's anointing is necessary for both and they can go together, as we see so clearly in Proverbs 31. Therefore, Heather never felt that she was just 'marking time' at home, waiting for a time when she could do something more important. For just as she knew that each child in the family was a gift from God, she also knew that the talents and abilities she had been given were to enable and equip her for that 'calling' as a mother and as a homemaker.

Matthew 25, verses 14-30 remind us all of the importance of using what God has given us, for here we see three men being entrusted with differing talents. The one who was given five talents used them to the full for increase and development, as did the one who was given two talents. And in using what they had been given they not only saw a hundred-fold increase but they were also put in charge of greater things. But the one who was given one talent, who hid it rather than using it, ended up in a position of total emptiness, when everything he had been given was taken away from him and given to the one who had made most use of all that had been entrusted to him.

Heather sought to live as a 'five talents' person seeking to develop what she had been given to the full, and as she did God certainly entrusted her with more.

"Multi-faceted, capable and confident to take up a challenge are words which spring to mind when I think of Mum," writes Julia. "Her willingness to have a go at almost anything was an inspiration to me. From my earliest memories of her, her willingness to encourage my creative play, to her determination to be productive by knitting Dad an Aran cardigan while she was in her last stages of illness, Mum demonstrated a thirst for knowledge, a flair for creativity and a production output which would be the envy of many factory outlets! Added to which were cookery, needlecraft, DIY, mechanics, many areas of interest, such as wildlife, music, literature, history . . . and the list goes on!

"Opportunity to develop my culinary skills came through Mum encouraging me to take responsibility for producing lunch on Saturdays whilst in my mid teens. Though a reluctant 'trainee,' due to lack of confidence in my abilities, I seem to remember we turned out some near edible dishes between us!"

Heather sought to live in her full inheritance in God and to pass whatever He had invested in her on to others, whether that be practical or spiritual. Joyce Sibthorpe, a family friend over many years, reminded me of the time when she and her husband Charles were moving into a deeper walk with God and used to call us for help and encouragement.

Joyce says, "I remember one time when I rang Heather to ask yet more questions and Julia answered the phone. When I asked her if I could speak to her Mum, Julia very confidently answered, 'Mum is seeking God and we are not allowed to disturb her.' For a moment I wondered if she was just having some peace and quiet. But I actually remember thinking, 'Is that what you are meant to do? To draw aside to hear from Heaven.' Heather did that at a time when David Abbott and other young men, plus her young children, were all living in the home. She spent time before the Throne of God. How I honour her for the priority she kept.

"From the time we first met, Heather had two teenagers and two little ones, who were the same ages as our own family. I had questions about child-raising, and constantly Heather inspired me because she was looking to the future. She was not looking for a quiet peaceful life, but she was training them. I can remember her talking as they went to school, helping them to see that they needed to aim for excellence; for God's favour on their lives. These were new concepts to me. I thought kids just grew up! But Heather realized that these qualities had to be developed, they didn't just happen. You have to train—and she trained them all. Today they all honour her for what she built into their lives."

Training your children according to the Word of God was something Heather taught and sought to model by the way she lived as a Mum. Proverbs 4, verse 23 speaks out the need to *guard your heart, for it is the wellspring of life.* We were very aware that instructing our children was more than just a matter of the words we used, for wrong attitudes in our hearts can so easily be transmitted to others, especially our children, and can leave them confused and hindered if not aligned to the Truth of His Word. One of our children, in paying tribute to Heather said, "Mum was real, she was encouraging and was always complimentary of others." I believe that such a testimony coming from her own family was because Heather taught from the unpolluted 'wellspring' of a guarded heart.

We were often asked the question in the course of our ministry together "What is your Church like?" Quite a normal question really, but I guess our answer was probably not so normal because we used to say "Come and stay in our home and you will see." We saw this as a very real invitation, not because we lived in a Church building, for we lived in a very ordinary home, but because Heather and I firmly believed that our homes should model Church as God intended it to be. They should be an example to others, a shop window if you like, of what it means to be 'family' together, reflecting all the dynamics of life that is ours to enjoy through the boundless love and forgiveness of our Heavenly Father.

Heather believed in the children and sought in every way to help them develop their full potential. This also meant giving them room to develop their own identities, their own ideas, how they dressed, the décor of their rooms (with some necessary limitations, of course!) and other such choices, for all these aspects bring expression of who they are. It meant helping them to feel very much part of the family by taking the risk of involving them in some appropriate decision making! It meant assuring them that she was always available to them *whenever*—and meaning it. It meant a willingness to share her life with them too, letting them into her heart, her disappointments, and her struggles, as well as her victories. Trying to project something which we are not is obvious to people who know us best, especially our family, for they soon see it as pretence and unreality. Heather was real in every way and she wanted to see that reality developed in our children by her own openness. She wanted the children to see her devotion to God and her total dependence on Him so she taught them how to trust Him in everything; how to pray; how to exercise faith; how to put His Word into action; how to love and serve Him.

In gratitude to her Mum, Julia wrote these words: "Mum's positive belief in us was special. To her there was nothing we couldn't do. She had high expectations of us which encouraged us to reach beyond mediocrity in studies and life's goals, and she took immense pleasure in hearing of our successes. I remember thinking about getting my results from various piano grade exams, and it almost not being in question that I would pass—which I usually did! Alternatively, if I didn't understand how to do something practical quite quickly Mum would be puzzled by my ineptitude!"

In our teaching to parents, Heather often used to say "Our children need to hear through our words and actions, 'I love you. I care for you. I want you to become God's maximum young man or young woman—and I am committed to you, for as long as you wish, to help you to be the best that God wants you to be. I will be praying for you. I will be here to counsel and guide you. I am prepared to make sacrifices, if necessary, to help you. All because you are important to me.'" We can't assume that they know these things, unless we express it to them.

Carlyn, a friend who trained with us on Team several years ago, and who is now an ordained Anglican minister who conducted Heather's Funeral Service in St. Austell, spoke of her qualities as a mother in this way:

"Each of Heather's five children were special to her in their own individual way. She was the proudest Mum in the Kingdom! She always made sure to praise every achievement, however small, as something they could personally be proud of, and whenever setbacks and disappointments came along she still found things to be positive about, encouraging them all the way and supporting them with her time and energy.

"With Heather the little things in the home were the big things. She took notice of her children's favourite food and was sure to cook it for them if they came round. She always wanted the best for her family—and she didn't rest until she had achieved it!

"Is it little wonder that, now Heather is no longer with them, her legacy of fine Christian family commitment to her children and grand-children has reached 'payback' time in the way they are now caring for their adored Dad and Grandad, Don. Yes, Don's family have been wonderful to him since Heather's death, but throughout their lives Heather had shown them the meaning of love in a family, the caring, the cherishing, the attention to quirky little details, and so much more, that all helped them to become strong individuals. Her tireless love and devotion firstly as a wife to Don, and then as a Mum and Grandma, all prepared the way for them to become loving, responsible adult children."

God doesn't have grand-children, not even in families that have a godly heritage which spans many generations, so the need for us to teach and show our children how to discover and develop their own personal relationship with God is so important and what a wonderful thing it is when they discover Jesus for themselves. Heather played a big part in all our children finding faith in Him for themselves and continued to help them so much along their own personal journeys of faith. When Simon, our son-in-law, brought tribute to Heather on behalf of Julia and himself at Heather's Thanksgiving Service, he said:

"Heather was an example of faith for she was one who feared the Lord—in the right way! She had a deep hunger for His Truth and desired to dig deep into His Word to find answers to life's questions. She was devoted to and raised her family in the same way. She was always looking and desiring for her children, grand-children and great grand-children to find God for themselves and to serve Him. She was proud of each one of them and always delighted in hearing of their achievements."

Although Simon never actually lived in our home as part of our 'extended family' he did spend a lot of his time with us as a family, so his gratitude of Heather is as a 'spiritual mother' as well as a mother-in-law. He writes:

"I am grateful for a woman who would always bring a richer understanding of God's Word. The Bible says that there are many teachers but few 'fathers'. I believe the same is true of 'mothers'. Heather was an amazing mother. She adopted Nigel and Julia into her heart and received, loved and raised them as her own. She became a spiritual mother who imparted so many precious things because she had faith in God, and us. Being a woman of the Word she was a great teacher who taught me so much. I say with a smile on my face 'she was a woman of strong opinions'. It was always interesting when Heather and myself were put together in the same room and we started to discuss issues!"

Heather was a knowledgeable woman who had an enquiring mind, so she always welcomed a healthy 'debate' with other strong believers as being helpful in firming up what she really believed. Many avoid such encounters, fearing that they will end up confused. But not Heather! For, whilst she was always ready to learn from others, she was not easily swayed by opinions that were not part of what she held as 'truth'. Her interests extended to a love of many other subjects, including wildlife, history and TV documentaries. Many would say that she also had an avid interest in crossword puzzles, but she saw these as an important exercise to keep her mind active as well as helpful relaxation. God made us as spirit, soul and body and it is important that we take time to do things that help to keep our whole being fit.

Many saw Heather as a hard worker, through which her creativity always shone through—especially at those special times. This obviously meant a lot to the family as Julia writes:

"Despite the stresses on her from many quarters, Mum always worked hard to make Christmas special for us. The little touches of hand-drawn name tags on our pillow cases of presents is something I remember being amazed by annually. I recall her late nights in sorting everything out and then producing eight, nine or ten masterpieces (usually colour co-ordinated), depending on how many people were living in the house at that time!"

Someone once wrote a popular song saying "little things mean so much". They certainly do, and for Heather they were all such a natural part of being the special 'mum' and 'homemaker' that she was.

First steps in learning how to live by faith

One of the most encouraging things for those of us involved in ministering to others is that of hearing testimonies from people who have taken hold of God's Word and proved the power of His promises for themselves. And it's particularly special when you see your own children exercising their own little 'mustard seed' faith and getting excited by God's answers. It was during a Mission at Ampthill, Bedfordshire, when our son Stephen was just three-and-a-half years old, that he desperately needed some new wellington boots for walking through the long wet grass on the tent site. Even at that young age Heather had taught him well about asking God for the things we need, so when bedtime came he didn't just ask Jesus for his wellington boots, he asked for red ones! Next morning Heather admitted that she had forgotten all about the boots, as she was due out at a coffee morning, but Stephen had chosen to stay with our hosts. When she came back for lunch a very excited little boy greeted her with such shouts of joy! "See what Jesus has given me." And there before us were his new wellingtons, and they were red ones!   He had begun to learn how to live by faith, trusting that God would supply his every need.

Another time when Stephen was thirteen years old, he was having to share a tent at our camps with Joel and Faith, his younger brother and sister. Now that he was growing up, he naturally wanted his own tent and his own space, but we had no means of buying one for him. Stephen realized this so, unbeknown to us, he prayed for his own tent. Some time later when we arrived home after being away together as a family, we unlocked the front door only to find a six-berth tent waiting for us in the hall. Again God had answered Stephen's prayer and supplied him with his own tent. It is always hard, especially as parents, when we face situations when we can't naturally provide for our children, but I believe that God allows such times to show us not only how dependent we are on Him, but also how just how eager He is to provide for us in abundance. Again I thank God for the way Heather faithfully taught the children life-application principles from the Word of God whilst I was away on ministry trips.

It has been very special for Heather and I to watch our children grow up through the various stages of childhood, adolescence and now into adulthood with spouses and families of their own, and to see their personalities and characters develop as God was honing them according to the gifts and callings He has planned for them. How we thanked God throughout all our years together for the privilege of being their parents, and for every opportunity to sow 'Kingdom seed' into their lives as we sought to nurture and train them in the ways of God, and to see the Holy Spirit water those seeds and bring forth fruit—for His glory.

As all parents will know, as our children grow and

change we need to grow and change too! Some of those changes are harder to face than others, but it is both challenging and exciting when God speaks into those situations with clear direction. It is rightly said that 'constant change is here to stay' and we fool ourselves if we think otherwise, because change is a necessary part of growth and new development. The natural world around us, which so clearly displays God's order, confirms that fact. For us, one such time of change, was early in 2005 when God called us to begin to 'step aside' from heading up our annual family camps and to hand on this 'baton' to our son Stephen and his wife Anne who had served so faithfully alongside us over a number of years, and whose own ministry gifts and leadership qualities were already in place. Whilst this was a big change for Heather and I to accept having founded these camps and seen them grow and develop over the years, seeing the next generation take on that 'baton' into the next stage of growth and development filled us with real joy and I have to say excitement too. I am so thankful that Heather has been able to see some of that new development happening under Stephen and Anne's leadership, and I honour them for the way they have continued to welcome our input and involvement whilst still embracing change.

Our children have not been special because of our ministry. They have still been children, and we have never wanted them to be anything but 'real'. With this desire, Heather and I agreed quite early on in our marriage that if ever our children were not coping with our life in ministry, with me away from home so often, then I would stop itinerating and even go back to a secular job if necessary. Incidentally, I firmly believe that secular work is still full-time ministry if that is what God has called us to, and we need to see our work place in that way. It should never be seen as a 'second-class calling', as we can still function there effectively (particularly as evangelists) and be right in the centre of God's will for us. However, we also believed that God's grace would be on our family and, because we knew He had called us, then He would also give our children grace to be able to live with that 'calling', with Abraham and Sarah being an example to us of those whom God calls He also equips.

But the time came when God tested the sincerity of our hearts in this, for one of our boys had a time of difficulty and God clearly told me to spend time with him whenever I was at home. You know when God speaks in that way prayer and trust are not enough, we also need to live out our promises so that our children (and God) know we mean what we say. Giving our son time in this way was a big lesson I needed to learn and through it God brought him through positively. Today he is a very solid Christian, secure in his own faith and developing his own ministry. One of the books which Heather and I went on to write is "Love is spelt T. I. M. E.", and time is never wasted if our hearts are set on raising our children for Him.

When our son Joel was just five years old at breakfast one day he asked Heather if he could have a banana. This was a very normal and healthy request, but the hard part was that she didn't have any, nor did she have any spare money as I was away at the time. Joel then asked Heather if she could buy some so he could have one when he got home from school. Perhaps a very obvious solution from a five-year old, but Heather then had to explain that as she had no spare money 'so we will have to ask Jesus to give us some so that I can buy bananas'. After doing just that as a family together, the children went off to their schools and, quite miraculously, when the post came later that morning a letter arrived with some money enclosed! Obviously Heather was then able to go out and buy Joel his bananas ready for when he came home from school. At the same time she was able to explain to him that the bananas were there because Jesus had sent some money in answer to his prayers. Joel has always been quite a deep thinker and Heather often recalled that moment as he sat quietly on his chair at the table eating his banana, and of how he looked up at her and calmly asked, "How did Jesus send the money. Did he open up the sky and drop it down?" It was a great opportunity to teach him how we can hear God prompt us to do things for others, and this is how the money came. Heather often recounted the situation she was in when faced with such a simple 'please Mummy can I have' request, and I am so grateful for the way she handled it to teach the children how to trust God.

In all that Joel went on to experience as he grew up in the family and moved into his own adult life, I am sure that every time he eats a banana he will remember God's answer to his trusting prayer. And now that he and Emma are parents themselves of five young children, no doubt, even to a Bank Manager, Heather's teaching will be remembered with gratitude and passed on to their own children. And I often wonder what other 'gems' may have been passed on from Mum to son as Joel spent some of the final hours of Heather's life alone with his very special Mum. She certainly shared her inheritance right to the end.

Heather always sought to model what she believed and her life-application teaching meant a lot to our children. Our daughter Faith writes:

"Mum was a great example to me and she taught me loads about how to be a 'Mum'. One example which was the best ever and great to see, even to the last weeks of her life, was her relationship with God. She was always reading her Bible and praying for us, the family and friends. Mum never hid away during those times so she showed us as a family how important it was to have a devotional time with God. I know it was a great joy to her when she knew her grand-children had given their lives to Him. I remember the time when our first child, Isaac, gave his life to the Lord. He was very young, but Mum encouraged me and Isaac believing that it doesn't matter what age you are if you love Jesus. She would have been so pleased to know that her other grandson, (our younger son, Ethan), also gave his life to the Lord just a few months after she died."

But it was not only the spiritual foundation that Heather sought to build into the family. She also saw the importance of training them to be future 'homemakers' in their own right. This is something which Faith so obviously appreciated as she paid tribute to Heather:

"When I was in my childhood," she writes, "Mum sat down with me and taught me how to do cross-stitch, sewing and knitting. She was very talented and creative and always had a needlework project on the go, either to have in the house or to give away. Mum made me two wonderful cross-stitch pictures, one for a 'Wedding Day' gift, and one when our first child, Isaac, was born. They now have pride of place on our landing at home, and its great to have wonderful treasures like that which a loving Mum created, just for me!

"Mum loved cooking and she loved to try different things and experiment with different foods. She taught me how to cook too by showing me what to do, and we had great times in the kitchen when I was a child. I remember on my 13th birthday we cooked a 13-course meal together! We had a great time experimenting with various recipes, and although the kitchen got in a bit of a mess it was great fun and Mum was there alongside to encourage and support me.

"Even when David and I got married, Mum and Dad said to us 'We won't interfere with your marriage, but we are here if there is anything you need.' We have never known them to interfere in any way, but they have always been there for us as we have asked for their support. Mum was such an example. Her support and help meant so much to me when we had the boys, and she encouraged me in how to handle the various situations which I faced as a new 'Mum' myself. She loved being around the boys and it was great to see her giving the gift of her time to them. When they were young, even into the last year of her life, they would sit on her lap as she read to them, encouraged them in some art work, or solved some puzzles with them —something which she always loved doing herself!

"Mum and I loved going shopping together. Even after I got married we always went Christmas shopping together every year before I moved away. It was a great 'Mum and daughter' time. If you knew Mum you will know that she loved shopping, but then don't all of us ladies love it too if we are honest! She always wanted me to have nice things that somehow expressed the relationship we shared together—which meant a lot to me."

Growing up to be a friend

Heather used to speak a lot in her teaching to parents about the phases we go through in our parenting roles, and of the need embrace change as our children move from childhood dependence and grow up to become mature young adults. With those phases comes a change of relationship between child and parent, and Heather always encouraged parents to not always seek to be an 'authorative figure' but to become a friend. It is a wonderful thing when our children become our friends, and when we can express mutual respect for each other. This meant a lot to Faith as she recalled what Heather meant to her:

"When I was growing up she was a great Mum, but as I got older our relationship turned from being just a 'mother and daughter' relationship to that of friends. Over the last few years of her life there were a few things which Mum bought me that showed this, the most memorable being that of a cushion on which was written, 'A daughter is a little girl who grows up to be a friend.'"

Heather sought to become a friend to all our children, with a listening ear tuned to encourage and support them in whatever they did. Someone once described encouragement as 'oxygen to the soul' and Heather wanted to help produce that pure air for them to breath, realizing that the world around is filled with so much pollution. And encourage she did, with great enthusiasm and creativity! She didn't stop at anything if it would bless and encourage. Those little personal touches that conveyed 'I love and appreciate you' remain so very special to our children and also to our grand-children. For Heather's love for each one of our fifteen grand-children always found expression in ways that would convey personal encouragement to them. She loved to have fun with the grand-children and this often found expression in making things for their school events. A wide variety of Christmas hats and fancy dress costumes spring to mind as I think about Heather's activities with them. Also the day when Heather and Jacob dressed a pony as a reindeer, with Jacob being 'Father Christmas'. They really went to town making the costume and had such a fun time together producing it all. I guess it is those little things that help to make the memory of a 'Mum' and 'Grandma' precious beyond words.

A close friend

One of the great books of the Old Testament is that of Ruth. It is one in which we read of the times of joy and sadness which Naomi and Ruth faced together along life's journey, and one which highlights the very special 'in-law' relationship which they shared together, for it speaks of an honouring of each other through commitment. When Heather and I moved to our new home in recent years we found ourselves in an area quite close to our son Stephen and his wife Anne and their family. For many years they have been very closely involved with us in *Good News Crusade* and we honour them for their commitment and support in so many areas of life and ministry. Indeed, all our family have been such a blessing to us. How good it is to be able to know such good 'in-law' relationships with each other, too, when we live in an age where there is often more ridicule and lack of respect than honour and appreciation.

Our daughter-in-law, Anne, in paying tribute to Heather, shares:

"Over many years Heather (known to me as Mum) has called me her best friend. She was, in fact, a very close friend and this developed from the very first days I knew her when I was just 16. Heather was not perfect by any means, but nevertheless she was a special, lovely and unique lady. I will never forget what she did for our children in their early lives. She devoted herself to them daily as I went to work. However, one day she forgot she had Josh and arrived at the GNC Office without him! When I asked where he was she said, 'Oh no, he is asleep. He is so good I forgot he was there.' Needless to say she rushed straight back home again, only to find him still fast asleep! She was a brilliant 'child-minder' though and gave them both such a great start in life. They were beyond their years once they started school, because she taught them so much. She was a lovely Nanny too. Even the day she died she was talking to Josh, and he promised he would see her soon. Because of that promise he actually did go and see her in the Chapel of Rest, which was quite an emotional time for me and him. Heather was very special to them.

"I so value the relationship Heather and I shared. I could say anything to her (and Don) and I knew that our relationship would not be jeopardized. They always knew that I loved them unconditionally. I had to share some very painful things with her, even during her last few months. It was very hard as I loved her dearly, but sometimes love hurts.

"I will always be grateful for those days that I nursed Heather; when I needed to do everything for her. Those of you who knew her would know that she was an independent strong woman who so disliked being dependent on someone else. Very much like me, I guess! But I remember God clearly saying to me that He wanted me to devote myself to her in her last days, for however long that would be. She was often apologizing for the things I had to do. For me it was a privilege and one that I will never ever regret. The day before she died I was washing her feet. But wasn't this one of the last things that Jesus did for His disciples too!

"Looking back on those times I am so grateful to God that I had those times with Heather. I would not have wanted it any other way. My family were incredible during those months and so supportive. They just knew that I had to do this for their Nanny and she often thanked them for allowing me the freedom to be with her. Steve, Josh, Jacob our adopted son Tom and Nigel and Barbara's son Phil (who lives and works with us) ran the home when I wasn't there, even having dinner on the table, and a glass of wine poured—waiting for me when I would eventually walk in!

"There are countless experiences I could share, but they are personal and precious to me. The emotional 'roller-coaster' that I was on was one that I wouldn't wish on anyone, but now I understand what others go through during such times. I miss Heather terribly. I often walk into the home and think I can smell her, hear her and expect her to walk into the room, but sadly she doesn't. She was indeed a uniquely special lady who will never be forgotten."

A family blended and extended!

There have been many who have shared our home and family life with us over the years and Heather and I, together with our children, have embraced that privilege together as God has brought them to us. The first member of our 'extended family' was David Abbot who shared a room with our son Nigel all the time he lived at home with us, that is from when he was fifteen until he was 21 years of age. And Simon Matthews (now my son-in-law), whose widowed mother lived just outside St. Austell, was often present as an extended family member. All these boys became great friends and enjoyed doing things together.

Paying tribute to Heather, David said,

"When I moved in with Don and Heather my life was in a real mess. I was young and didn't know how to do anything—not even toasting bread! I wanted to be loved, but was afraid so I would reach out and when response came I would run—and sometimes I was quite verbal too. This went on for several years before I was free.

"Stephen was just two years old when I moved in, and Joel and Faith were born while I was living there. Heather had to teach me how to care for babies and then she astounded me by trusting **me** *to baby-sit. The 'trust thing' she had just bowled me over because even when I couldn't give or receive love with adults I could with children, and Heather trusted me. Stephen used to want to go everywhere I went, riding on my shoulders, until he went to school. Often this involved him in being away with me for some hours, but if Stephen wanted to go, Heather would usually let him.*

"I remember being amazed at the wisdom Heather had in dealing with the needs of her own children. Christmas was always a big thing in the 'Double'

family, and I spent every Christmas with them until I got married. Heather quite rightly taught the children that it was Daddy who put the presents at the bottom of their beds. However, the first Christmas Eve after Stephen started school he went off to bed but in a short time was crying and screaming in panic. Heather rushed into him and soon discovered that he was scared because he had been told at School that 'Father Christmas' brought the presents and he was frightened because he didn't want a stranger coming into his bedroom! Heather gently talked and prayed with him and then left his room with Stephen calm and peaceful. He immediately went off to sleep and didn't wake until the morning.

"Another time we were short of money in the run up to Christmas and although Heather had made her Christmas cake, she didn't have money to buy the icing sugar to finish it off. Being the creative person that she was, and rising to the challenge, she took some granulated sugar which she had in the cupboard and ground it up in her electric mixer, thus producing fine sugar to ice her cake! Heather's parents were due to be with us on Boxing Day and her father loved Christmas cake, so much so that to him no Christmas was complete without it! We hadn't eaten any of the cake on Christmas Day so this untouched specimen was brought out for Dad and us to enjoy. But when Heather went to cut the cake the home produced icing had set so hard—like concrete in fact—that nothing or no one could even dent it. So a much-embarrassed Heather summoned up yet more creativity and promptly turned the cake upside down cutting it from the base, much to the amusement of everyone. But the cake was lovely!

"Heather was someone who knew how to give; her

time, her love, her help. A need expressed became an opportunity to give or to provide it on a long-term loan. If she'd got it she gave it!

"I have many special memories of my time with Don and Heather, not least the help they gave me as I approached my Wedding Day, for it was Heather who organized that whole day for us. Yet she had the amazing ability to do it in such a way that it appeared like my ideas — and that I was doing the organizing! Then Heather happily sat back and let me take all the credit — never even hinting to anyone, even up to when she died, what she had actually done for us. What a servant heart she had! A very special person who had a big place in my heart, for 47 years ago she took me into her heart and treated me just like one of her own family."

It was Heather's big heart for God that enabled her to embrace all whom she knew God had sent to share our family, her one desire being to love them as her own for however long their stay with us would be. Many have echoed the words that she was a natural 'homemaker extraordinaire! '

Andrew Batstone is another one who enjoyed family life with us for a number of years as he worked as part of our GNC support team, particularly on the technical side. Quite amusingly, he too recalls Heather's great cooking, "well everything that made it to the table!", he adds. "The dog enjoyed many a great meal that never quite made the grade, for she had her standards! But, as they say, practice makes perfect!"

A memory of Heather that will always stay with Andrew is this:

"On the subject of a perfect woman who rises early, how well I can bear witness to the fact that Heather was an early riser, doing much of her teaching and preaching preparation very early in the day before anyone else was around vying for her attention. I can still vividly remember being rudely awakened at 6.30 in the morning to the strains of Heather quickly running the vacuum cleaner around outside my room." Fond memories, nonetheless, from one who knew what it was to enjoy the fun side of our family, for Heather saw this as bringing a necessary balance to the life we all shared together.

Robert Parkinson, now a Baptist Minister, also lived with us for two years and worked with us on Team.

His memories of Heather during that time with us are of "a warm and welcoming person who made my living with them a real pleasure. Lots of people came in and out of the home but Heather was the constant presence who kept everything running. She was, of course, also the attentive mother of their own children, as well as Don's support, strength, soul-mate and organizer, but somehow she seemed to be able to harness everything together, including cooking delicious meals, often for large groups of people as well as her extended family.

"Heather was the kind of person you could always talk to, and she seemed to care about everyone's interests, being keen to make sure that they were happy. She was a peacemaker and a friend who always showed genuine interest in whatever others were doing. I was constantly reading books and, being an avid reader herself, Heather was always keen to learn what I was reading about too. She was a great conversationalist and always had her finger on the pulse of the Christian scene. But perhaps one of the memories that sticks in my mind is that of the odd quiet evening when we sat in front of the 'telly' watching show jumping together! Yes, for those of you that didn't know, Heather did actually quite enjoy this once regular feature on BBC2!"

Many others who spent time as part of our 'family' and worked on Team with us now have very fruitful international ministries themselves, two of those being Dr. Peter Gammons and Jonathon Conrathe. Peter lived with us for around five years and during that time he says:

"I saw what a Christian couple should be, for everything they preached they practised in the home. Heather was amazing, releasing Don to travel extensively to fulfil God's call. She saw it as a ministry. Every night we would sit down to some good home-cooked food, pray and read the Scriptures together. Heather herself was a great teacher of the Word and always had her Bible in her hand looking for something new.

"But don't get the idea that Heather was always serious, for she was a real practical joker too. Like the time when she persuaded me to try a spoonful of Tabasco sauce which I was convinced was soup! All good fun though and part of what made Heather a brilliant friend and homemaker."

For Jonathon, coming from quite a sheltered Surrey background, moving into our home and living as part of family was quite a culture shock. As family we have always been quite frank and open in our communications with each other, and Jonathon recalls his initial experiences when he moved in with us.

"I found Heather to be a very frank and open communicator. Whilst this may sound a bit of a negative statement, I actually look back on some of her comments to me as a young evangelist as being quite impacting and life-changing. I remember her saying, 'Jonathon, you must come to the place where neither the approval or rejection of others means anything to you, but only that you have done the will of God.' Another time was when I just wanted some time out from evangelism to just be 'normal' (whatever that is!). Again Heather's words stick in my memory for she said, 'Jonathon, you must accept the fact that from the time God called you, you ceased to be 'normal'. You will never be 'normal' again!' Just two examples of Heather's powerful 'kitchen-sink sermonettes!

"Heather was an amazingly creative woman, who always had some beautiful 'stitch-craft' or other art expression on the go. As I wandered around the house I often used to stop and admire such beautiful work. Other household activities included cooking up some gastronomic delight; doing the accounts for Don, sitting studying Scripture or counselling someone over coffee. She was certainly not one to stand still for long, and many times exhibited a tremendous compassion for people who were in genuine difficulties.

"In the home, one of the things that stood out so obviously was her total commitment to her family. They were, next to God, her number one propriety. Though she was a very able and interesting teacher of the Word, with quite a prophetic edge to her ministry, she seemed to accept her responsibilities to be at home for the children's sake with remarkable grace. I watched her spend many hours just sitting with them, sometimes watching a movie, sometimes just chatting or playing a game, and, after the evening meal, gathering the family round the table for 'family devotions' in just the same manner as Don did when he was at home.

"I observed first-hand, Don and Heather's walk of faith when there was not enough money to pay the bills, or when they really needed extra finance to do some extension work on the property, or when the children were asking for something they couldn't afford. Sometimes they gathered the family around the table but always they simply prayed for the provision they needed, thanked the

Lord and then went happily along trusting as if the money were already there. And it always came. Such was their faith in God's promises. They taught all their children to tithe and give, and if they wanted something which Don and Heather could not afford the answer was not 'no'. It was, 'you better go and talk to Jesus about that.' Discipleship certainly began in the home, both through teaching and example.

"It is now 13 years since I left the Team and moved back to Surrey where 'Valley Ministries' was birthed, and in all those years never once has Heather ever failed to send me a birthday or Christmas card from them both, even up to her final Christmas on this earth. One amazing and lovely woman of God, and I thank God for the privilege of being part of their family for three years."

I guess that this book would be volumes long if everyone whose life God touched through Heather's ministry in our home included their own tributes to her, for there are certainly many more who echo similar life qualities and memories which have impacted them and helped them to pursue a deeper walk with God—and others who have been called into ministry themselves in different parts of the world. However, these tributes would be incomplete if I didn't also take this opportunity of expressing my gratitude to all those who have shared family life with us in our home over the years, for Heather and I were always so aware that it was certainly not just us doing the giving. Every one that came to share our home with us for a season God used to help bring His 'honing' to our lives too, and we were made the richer in Him and more usable in His service through all who shared their lives with us.

Family life is a very precious thing to share together and it is something which we all need to contribute *to* and play our part *in*, in the **secure** knowledge that we are totally loved and accepted. And within those relationships we need tolerance and understanding *of* each other and patience *with* each other if we are to truly live God's way. For we each need to know how to relate and respond to each other; how to lean *on* each other and find support *from* one another; how to give and receive *from* each other; how to confess *to* another and find forgiveness *from* them and to learn to *release* one another and yet still find each other *dependable*.

For Heather and I seeking to live as a family in this way, whilst being involved in full-time ministry, has meant that our children have been very much in the public eye and have needed to share us as parents with many others across the world. Whilst in the main they have seen this as a privilege, it has also had its sacrificial aspects which have been harder to handle. The seemingly untimely passing of Heather as 'Mum' to some of our family has brought a real awareness of that costly sharing over the years, I want to honour each one of our children as individuals, for the way they have embraced life within our family and been so supportive in all that God called us to throughout their lives. When working through your own loss, as many of you will know, it is not always easy to reach into the wells of precious personal memories and make those public too, but I trust that the tributes shared bring a real awareness of a much loved Mum, the memory and appreciation of whom could never ever be forgotten nor fully expressed in words.

5

A Faithful Friend

A friend loves at all times
Proverbs 17:17

Love does not say *give me* but let *me give you*.
—Jill Briscoe

One of the principles of life that the Lord has impressed on us over the years was that *people matter more than things*. How true this is. It is so easy to fill life with so many things (even good things), that there is little time left to relate to people. A life bereft of friendship is a sad one. Heather had the amazing ability of treating people as friends and helping them to feel valued and loved. She always started from what God says in His Word from the time of creation—for there we can see that we were formed to share a personal, intimate and living relationship with Father God— enjoying friendship with Him, and a sense of belonging to each other too.

A cartoonist once depicted a man being held up by a thief, who grabbed the victim's hands, pushed a sack into them and then shoved them into his chest saying, 'ere, put all valuables in this.' The next frame showed the man eagerly trying to pack his friends into the sack! Friends are indeed a valuable asset and that is how Heather saw each one. I guess if she had been the one in the cartoon she might have tried to do the same thing! You only have to read through Heather's personal journals which she kept to see just how much she treasured her friends, for she saw them as gifts from God. Their concerns became her concerns; their joy, her joy; their prayers and praise— her prayers and praise! Her wisdom and godly counsel was always given with compassion from Father's heart, and many walk strong in God today because of her loving input and caring faithfulness.

With Heather's open heart came the invitation of an open home, and many speak of the warmth and acceptance they found through the expression of Heather's love in our home. A lovingly prepared meal, a word of encouragement, a card or some hand-crafted gift, a welcome stay in our home, a listening ear during a walk in the park with our dogs *Honey* or *Petro*, a quiet sit in the garden, or simply sharing a 'cuppa,' all gave tangible expression of a friend who loved at all times. In fact, many would say it was impossible to leave our home without Heather also giving you something to take home with you!

Being 'a friend who loves at all times' means having a selfless attitude of heart. It requires great grace; grace to allow the fruits of the Holy Spirit to be cultivated and applied in a tangible way. It means so much to know that tender touch at a time when all around seems harsh and hostile; to know the warmth of a welcome hug when feeling so isolated; to be understood, even when not necessarily agreed with; or to have those phone calls last thing at night when you have lost a precious loved one, just to say "I have been praying for you. How has your day been today?" To be interested enough to listen, care, encourage and then pray for the tomorrow that needs to be faced. To have someone to say, "Night, Night. Sleep well. We love you", when going to sleep in an empty bed and a now silent room. To know that they are not just 'words' but real expressions of a heart that truly loves.

An over-flowing heart and filled hands!

All of these loving expressions flowed out so naturally from Heather's heart to others in need. Proverbs 31: 20 AMP says *She opens her hands to the poor, Yes, she reaches out her **filled hands** to the needy [whether in body, mind or spirit].* Those very ordinary hands of Heather's were indeed **filled hands** and through them the Lord brought peace—faith—hope—care—wisdom—encouragement—life . . . to countless numbers of people along the path of friendship.

Heather taught and gave 'encouragement' founded on the Word of God, which meant that if you were seeking a response such as, 'O, you poor thing' you didn't get it! She was certainly not one to put on the 'guest list' if you were thinking of who to invite to a 'pity party'! Instead she spoke faith and hope into people's hearts and situations and reminded afresh of the promises of God based on His Word. Proverbs 31: 26 says 'She speaks with wisdom, and faithful instruction is on her tongue.' This is the hallmark of a true friend and woman of God.

From the many tributes and cards we received as a family following Heather's 'home call' it is clear that Heather's friendship was valued by hundreds across the world, because she had the amazing ability to make each one feel special. Why? Because in an amazing way they did all have a special place in her heart. Friends have said that 'I felt loved, never judged.' 'She made you feel so special, even if you had not done anything noteworthy.' Her love was always genuine and sincere. Yes, of course, she had those she held as close friends, but never to the exclusion of others who needed her friendship too.

Heather sought to live her life in close relationship with

the Lord, knowing that it is only in that place of intimacy that we hear Father's clear heartbeat for ourselves, and often for those who are close to our heart too. It didn't matter what time of the day people popped in to see her at home, but sooner or later would come the phrase, "I was praying about this, and the Lord showed me . . ." or "I felt God say to me . . ." and then she would share wonderful insights from her own walk with the Lord. How this strengthened the faith of so many!

At Heather's Thanksgiving Service at the 'Good News Crusade Family Camp' in Taunton, Anne Trahearn, a friend of many years who served closely with Heather on ministry trips at home and abroad, spoke of a number of aspects of Heather's friendship for which she will always be grateful to God, not least the affirmation and challenge which she brought to her, and many others, through the title of this book! *Course You Can!* spoken in her lovely Cornish accent, was encouragement that readily came from Heather's heart and lips to those who were hesitating on taking a new step (or stride!) into something new that God was asking them to do. Her thinking was always, 'Why should we doubt God's enabling when He has chosen to use us and take us beyond our own ability—into His?' And she was right!

Some of our closest friends over the years have naturally been those who became part of the GNC team and others who have worked closely with us in ministry. Among those have been Mike and Muriel Darwood, who themselves moved to Cornwall and lived just round the corner from us when we lived in Poltair Road. Muriel went to be with the Lord in recent years, after her own battle with cancer, but Mike writes:

"The first time we met Don and Heather was in November 1965, when we had been saved only a few weeks. They were on a mission in Godmanchester in

John and Rhoda Martin—
Heather's parents

Heather's Dad in
naval uniform

Baby
Heather

Heather with older
brother Brian

oung Love!—
the engaged
couple

Wedding Bells! 1964

The young
Double fami[...]
reunited

Family Group: Stephen, Don,
Nigel, Julia, Joel,
Heather and Faith

One of Grandma Heather's first prize
creations for a Pony Club event

Ruby Wedding Celebration May 2004—Group photo of grand-children

Inset: Don and Heather on their special day

Tabora

Singida

TANZANIA

K

Bicycles

Sewing machine

Aid provided for 'He
for the Handicappe
Tanzania 2004

INDIA

TAMIL NĀDU

Valparai

āladi

Bodināyakkanūr

Periyakulam

Allinagaram

Madu

KERALA

Kamham

Erāttupetta

Tiruvalla

Heather
ministering in India

Construction of playground
area and equipment Uganda

Ministry trip to Jinja, Uganda

Left: Kahoya Champion's Academy in Eldoret,
Kenya—A classroom in Heather's memory

Above: An Evangelism Training Course
in Eldoret, Kenya 2005

A Woman of the Word

Heather and *Petro*

Heather ministering at Ladies' Conference

Don and Heather leading tour in Israe

Cambridgeshire and it was the first time that the then mission tent was being used. We met Don and Heather at a mission meeting being held in nearby Hartford, Huntingdonshire (now Cambridgeshire), where Don was preaching and Heather was playing the organ, and it was at those meetings where we were both baptized in the Holy Spirit.

"In 1966 Don and Heather came back to our area — this time to St. Ives in Huntingdonshire (now Cambridgeshire) — to conduct another mission, and we invited them to stay in our home, giving over our bedroom for them to use for the three-week period. The first night Heather was restless and didn't sleep at all well, which was apparently unusual for her. When they came down for breakfast the next day I asked the usual 'host' question, "Did you sleep well?" Heather, being the honest person that we soon discovered she was said, "No, not really. I was kept awake by your clock ticking." "But we haven't got a clock in the bedroom", I said. "You must have" Heather argued, "because it was definitely a loud ticking." The mystery was solved when we discovered that it was in fact the Lloyd-loom chair in our bedroom which was found to be infested with woodworm, and their 'activity' did resemble the loud and continuous ticking of a clock! Needless to say it was duly removed from the house, taken outside and destroyed by fire — and Heather slept happily ever after during her stay, and during many other visits to our home which followed over the years.

"We were both involved with Don and Heather in putting the tent up, and in painting poles, etc. in those early days of missions, for it really was a case of all hands on deck! But it was the beginning of 'team' building and partnering together in the work of the

Gospel. We became great friends through those times together and had great fun too, not least when Heather and Muriel attempted to use our temperamental twin-tub washing machine together, which certainly had a mind of its own, and brought them much amusement, lightening the load of wash days!

"On one occasion it was Don's birthday during their stay with us. We had a South African man staying with us too. Many of you will know of Don's great love of strawberries, so we traditionally produced some for a treat with our 'afternoon tea'. Heather offered to make everyone a cup of tea and politely asked our South African guest if he would like a cup. I guess he had summed us all up by then, so felt he could join in the fun, because he said 'No thanks. I'd like a bucket of tea!' Needless to say, Heather took him at his word, filled the nearest bucket and then dared him to drink it. After much fun, he eventually declined consuming this amazing 'cocktail,' but he did eat the strawberries!

"Don and Heather stayed with us lots in those early days of GNC ministry and we went on to enjoy many years of friendship and fun as we worked together, especially when we re-located to Cornwall. They regularly sought to bless us through invitations to their home where we enjoyed rich fellowship together. We so appreciated Heather's loving care and concern for us, and of course the lovely meals she always prepared.

"As I have continued to share meals with Don and Heather since dear Muriel died in 2005, I have often taken one of my poems to them in appreciation. With my increasing blindness, Heather was very touched by the depth of revelation God brought through them, so much so that she was keen to see these new ones *published for the blessing of others too. This meant adding a sixth poetry book to the five that were already in print (thanks to the help of Tim Jones). Heather, being the creative person that she was, had the idea of illustrating these new poems with appropriate clip art, and as they say 'he who gets the vision gets the job,' so she took the initiative to produce my latest book of poems , entitled 'Harvest Promise'. She was able to get it published in record time not long before she died. Heather's gift of friendship always looked for opportunities to promote and honour others and I thank the Lord for every precious memory of her."*

With Mike's permission I share one of his poems, which became a favourite of Heather's.

Harvest Promise

The last few globules
Of green sourness
Are slowly yielding
To the gentle caresses
Of the autumn sun.

One by one they change their dresses
For red robes,
And prove their ripeness
By yielding to my outstretched hand.
Grateful, perhaps
That I did not leave them
To rot on the vine.

Dear Lord, great Gardener,
Watch over me still,
Until I ripen,
And you gather me
Into your store.

For many years another dear friend, Dr. Tony Stone,

served on the Council of Reference of GNC. Along with his wife Sheila, their recollections of Heather could best be summed up in who she was as a person: "Yes, an amazing woman of God, but one with a unique blend of qualities that left an impression on others lives." They recognized Heather's sincere devotion and total support to me and the whole household that made up our 'family' and, like so many others, appreciated the genuine warmth of Heather's welcome and love expressed to guests in our home.

None would argue with the fact that she was a woman of strength who called 'a spade a spade' and not 'an agricultural implement', but from a heart that sought only to live in reality and honesty came an equally strong and steely determination to face every situation, good or bad, with the a desire that God would be honoured through it, whatever the cost. As the phrase goes, Heather did not 'suffer fools gladly', but in all the many years that Tony and Sheila knew her they confess that they never heard her speak negatively of anyone, hence her compliments were precious and seen as so much more genuine and honest.

Many friends have spoken of Heather as their 'role model' and this was echoed by Joyce Sibthorpe (a friend over many years) who paid tribute at Heather's Thanksgiving Service at our Taunton Family Camp last year. Joyce and her husband Charles first met Heather and I in 1969. Heather was just 25 years old at the time and Joyce, who was a few years older, recognized her even then as 'a giant in God' and thought of the Scripture in 1 Timothy, 4:12 *Don't let anyone look down on you because you are young, but set an example for the believers in speech, in life, in love, in faith and in purity.* She saw someone she wanted to learn from and someone she wanted to follow as she journeyed with God—and she did!

On many occasions, Joyce would travel from Redruth

to St. Austell to talk with Heather and to seek answers for her many questions, and she always found Heather so welcoming, so loving, so patient, so kind and so helpful. Although Joyce had come from a Church background that would have put her in the 'enemy Camp' as far as teaching on the Holy Spirit was concerned, Heather always welcomed and accepted her. This meant so much to Joyce and Charles, particularly as their attitude towards us before their fresh encounter with the Holy Spirit had been more of suspicion than acceptance! Only God can break down those walls that seek to divide and then transform them into bridges to cross into each others lives; bridges that enable such precious friendships to develop. What a testimony to His amazing grace and mercy!

One of Charles and Joyce's lasting memories of Heather was that of her generous hospitality. Joyce writes:

"We never went to Don and Heather's home, invited or uninvited, without actually receiving abundance. I had tended to think that God was a bit stingy, but then I went to Don and Heather's one Christmas and thought 'Wow, this is just like Paradise!' We walked into an abundance of love, joy, gifts and fun in that home. My lasting memory is that of going on a ministry trip with Colin Urquhart and going to Don and Heather's home. Heather served up raspberries from the garden—and not just raspberries, but an explosion of raspberries, topped with a choice of cream; single, double, Cornish, Greek yoghurt and ordinary yoghurt! I think that sums up the Heather we knew. She lived life to the full, and sought to give in abundance to others too."

I guess it was a real surprise to me at Heather's 'Thanksgiving Service' to learn how God had used Heather so much in Joyce's life, and it made me realize how important it is to live a godly life as we don't always know who is seeing us as a 'role model' and following our example as a pathway to a deeper walk with Him.

Keith Archer and his wife Carol reminded me of the first time they met us, and of the impact Heather's prayer ministry had on their lives. Keith writes:

"It was at one of the early GNC Camps at Blaithwaite House in Cumbria and we had by-passed the idea of camping, opting for the comforts of the house! Those of you who know anything about GNC Camps will know that people are always placed in 'units' to enable a smaller group of people to get to know each other, and you didn't escape this arrangement even in the house! We found ourselves, therefore, in the same 'unit' as the Doubles and the GNC team. Not what we had bargained for when we booked! It also meant sharing meal times, sitting at tables with different ones in order to get to know each other. It all felt a bit vulnerable!

We got through to the Monday without too much interaction and then learned that there was an 'Eve's Meeting' planned for teatime that evening. Obviously it was a time for the ladies, with the intention that the Dads would get the tea and put the children to bed. I felt a bit smug about this as we had no children, so while everyone else was busy I could opt out and rest on the bed, which I did. Later, when Carol came back and I asked her how the meeting went, she just smiled coyly. It had obviously been a special time, but I was not too sure that I wanted to know why, so I didn't press her for information. Later on that evening Carol told me that Heather and Muriel Darwood had called her over to them at the end of the meeting, apparently because they had sensed that I didn't like children and they needed to pray with her—and for me! How could they know this, I thought, because up to this point we hadn't even been at their tables for meals or had a conversation with either Heather or Muriel. But what they were thinking was right, and I was amazed at Heather's discernment.

"Needless to say that prayer was answered, and to mine and Carol's delight very soon a baby was on the way. But there was more, as, because Heather rightly discerned, I was not planning to be there at the birth. It was not such a common practice in those days so I saw it as Carol's time! More prayer followed, and again God's answer came! I became very eager to be there and didn't want to miss it—but feared that I might as I was working away from home at the time in Holland. However, God knew how much I needed to be there, so He saw to it that I made it back in time to share the miracle of God's gift to us through our eldest daughter Jo-Ann's birth. Great rejoicing followed, and we even had a prayer meeting around the bed with two of the Christian midwives!

"Being so delighted with God's gift of Jo-Ann, (meaning Yahweh's gracious gift), I prayed for another just like her and guess what, God heard that prayer too. Almost three years later Ruth was born into our family. What a joy these girls have been to us—and now a granddaughter too. And what amazing answers God brings when He highlights a need for breakthrough prayer. Carol and I even ended up running a Children's Club on our estate for several years for other people's children too —and also a Pathfinder Group with 40 children.

"Carol and I, together with our family, are so grateful to God for Heather's life, friendship and her prayer ministry. She certainly had His discernment and knew how to pray for breakthrough in our lives, and we are sure that countless others can testify to the effectiveness of her prayers too."

Keith and Carol Archer's friendship links with us have grown and developed over the years and with that has come their active involvement in the life and work *Good*

News Crusade. Keith was, for a number of years, Chairman of our Trustee Board and also one of our Camp Pastors, so he has obviously become a regular part of our more 'official' meetings. It was here where he saw what a multi-faceted woman Heather was and he was struck with the way God had given her such compassion for people as ministry and mission were considered, balanced with such a clear, incisive mind and extremely good administrative skills on the 'business' side of GNC, where those skills were needed for strategy and resourcing. He always enjoyed those moments around our meal table, too, when Heather would share with him some insight she had received from God's Word or she would talk over her latest project, the latter never ever being in short supply, as wherever Heather was there was a project either happening—or about to!

None were probably closer to knowing Heather from day-to-day, though, than George and Esther Dennis who have served us in the home for many years and what a tremendous gift they are from the Lord. They have such willing hearts to be to us whatever we need them to be, that nothing has ever been too much trouble. What a wonderful living tribute to honestly be able to say about friends! During our cancer journeys they were a marvellous practical support and with Esther's training, her nursing care and support was so appreciated too. Through their availability to us we have become great friends over the years, and thankfully through this relationship we have been able to give back to them too.

Heather often spoke of the way that she knew the Lord had called and appointed her to a 'ministry of helps' listed in 1 Corinthians, 12:28 and Esther was one who appreciated Heather's practical ministry. For, as well as so many other things, she taught her to read, write and spell. As we all know, these very basic skills form the foundation for further development and learning, and they certainly did for Esther as she went on to train in the care and nursing of others. Heather was also able to teach her how to sew and enjoy other aspects of needlework. Again, another basic skill, but one which helped Esther to develop and use these gifts in the home and family, as well as for her own achievement and pleasure.

An amusing time which Esther recalls is when she and Heather used to look after the grand-children together. Often the respective parents would phone when they were on their way to collect the children. Realizing that it would probably be them on the end of the phone they would answer by saying 'Chinese laundry' or 'Crèche service!' However, one day the caller was not a 'parent' but a local Minister who promptly apologized because he thought he had dialed the wrong number! It was not the last time that this experience happened either.

Another time, when we were living at Poltair Road and kept the telephone by the front window, Esther recalls how she answered a call. Some time later, when another call came in, Heather looked for the phone and couldn't find it. A search began everywhere for this missing object but it wasn't found in any of the obvious places such as another room, drawers or cupboards. For a time it was bit like the woman recorded in Scripture who lost the coin. But unlike her it was one of those times when they just gave up looking for a while hoping that it would 'come to light'. Much to their amusement, later in the day this is just what happened for there in the fridge was the missing phone. It was of course very cold, but very soon became a hot line again!

It was Heather who helped George through problems he was facing in those early years, and who was subsequently involved in bringing him to know the Lord. Like so many, I guess, she will always have a special place in his heart because of this, and he misses her greatly. One of George's fondest memories of Heather is that of what became a parting gift to him, for in her final days of failing health she knitted him an Aran-style cardigan. He really treasures this as it is such a reminder of Heather's heart of love to give, and her desire to personally bless others right up to her last breath. What a testimony of His loving-kindness expressed through a treasured friend, a quality which just exuded from Heather as she related to people, for the warmth of her love enabled them to feel so accepted and affirmed as she drew them into her heart.

Proverbs 31, verse 26 says *She speaks with wisdom, and faithful instruction is on her tongue.* Heather took this Word very seriously, seeking only to be positive in her speech. Even when given the opportunity to gossip or speak negatively of others, she sought only to be factual and honouring and many a conversation that the enemy was seeking to take over and use was kept on a godly course and remained edifying.

Heather often used to say "friendships develop, they don't just happen". They require the giving of time to each other; time to confide, listen, understand, empathize, support, encourage . . . and Heather sought to develop friendships that embraced all these aspects, and more, without being fearful that people would, in the end, be time wasters. 'True friendship', it is said, 'is able to discern the motivation of the other person,' and Heather's discernment gave her the ability to clearly recognize people's motives and to leave them with wise counsel, without any sense that she was pushing them aside, because it was always her heart to take every opportunity to encourage and build faith in the *whosoevers*, just as Jesus taught.

It would be impossible to include the countless other testimonies we have received over the years of God's answers to Heather's discerning prayers, for she was one who saw the importance of being led by the Holy Spirit as she prayed. She wanted to see 'breakthrough' in people's lives and situations so she knew the importance of going for the 'jugular', as they say, and dealing with the root issues.

Her book, entitled *Ouch! That Hurt*, records so honestly the areas which the Lord highlighted as blockages in her own life, and the release He brought through specific 'breakthrough prayer'. Heather's honest testimony, spoken through the pages of this book, has helped thousands across different parts of the world to seek the Lord for His breakthrough in their lives too. It is a book which has been translated into different languages already, including Kirwandan, and it has been powerfully used, especially with the traumatized teenagers of the 1990's genocide, and even as I write it is being translated and printed in Swahili.

At this present time of so much unrest in Kenya, which in some ways is similar to the tribalism of Rwanda's past trouble, we are looking to provide as many copies as we possibly can of *Ouch! That Hurt* for these precious, traumatized people who have seen so many of their loved ones killed or maimed. Heather so loved the people of Kenya and interestingly she first preached the message and testimonies on which this book is based at a Leaders' Conference in Eldoret, where so much trouble has been centred. How Heather would have so wanted this message of her own testimony to continue to help these dear people to find security and freedom in Christ in their own lives—and the grace to forgive.

A life well lived

Dan Sneed, who has become a treasured friend and colleague over many years of ministering together, also paid tribute to Heather at her 'Thanksgiving Service' at our Taunton Family Camp last year.

"In listening to all the tributes given this morning, all the aspects of Heather's life could be summed up in one simple phrase 'A life lived well'. for even through her last months, when she 'fought life's final war with pain and suffering', she sought to live life well to the end. So many people (who represent so many more from across this nation and overseas), have repeatedly spoken of Heather as a very real person. One who was generous and kind in every way. One who was creative and inspiring. She had a very special laugh and was full of fun. Yes she was feisty and often opinionated, but she was also practical, positive and very honouring. She was a woman of prayer. A woman of the Word. A woman who had the fear of God in her life, in the right sense. But the phrase I most remember was 'Course you can!' for it really reflected Heather's heart as she moved through life and encouraged others to too."

Dan continues, "Two weeks ago I was sitting at breakfast with my Pastor, Jack Heyford. As we finished and walked out together to our cars he bent down to pick up a one penny piece which was lying on the ground. I thought, 'Why would a 73-year old man need to do that in a parking lot?' When he had picked up this coin he held it up and said, 'There is a sermon in everything. Did you ever read the parable about the penny which I wrote?' 'No' I said. Apparently it had been birthed in his heart when he had previously picked up another penny and God had spoken to him about 'the value of one'.

"One thing that was seen so clearly in Heather was her value of people, for whenever you were around her you knew you were valued. Today we are seeing something of Heather's value, and of what one person has done to touch the lives of so many people. Her life meant so much to all of us gathered here, but far beyond that to the thousands in other parts of the world who were also touched by God through her life. Why? All because she was open and willing to do what God wanted her to do. Not in any way to replicate herself, for she was one of a kind—a unique creation of God as we all are, but because she wanted to see others come into everything that God had for them too, and to live every moment of life in the fullest possible way.

"Heather was a real and transparent person. So real that you always knew that what you saw was what you would get! That's a compliment, for you never had any worries about a hidden agenda or what she might be thinking. You always knew! I never felt I had to appear to be perfect when I was around her. There are a lot of people who do make you feel that way, having to be on your guard not to say or do the wrong thing! But not so with Heather. In all the many years I have actually known both Don and Heather as we have shared together in their home, or ours, at camps and conferences or wherever, I have never felt that I had to be anything other than just myself. Our times together have always left me feeling really good, even if thoughts expressed were somewhat opinionated and direct, for Heather had such a way of relating that, although you may have thought 'that hit', God showed me that it was OK, it was helpful and I needed that. It was a gift from God that she had which communicated reality and truth.

"Colossians 3:23 says 'Whatever you do, work at it with all your heart, as working for the Lord'. Heather's zeal for the Lord meant that she put everything into everything she did — and it showed! I always loved to hear her speak. She had an incredible gift of imparting to others the revelation which God had given to her. She was real and practical, and was able to illustrate her teaching in such creative ways that enabled people to be drawn into what she was communicating, for she always wanted to reach their hearts, to get them involved, and to bring life-application help."

When speaking on relationships with others Heather always taught the vital key as being firstly that of our relationship with God, and of all other relationships radiating from ours with Him. That is how she lived, and the many tributes that friends have shared reflect that fact. It would be impossible to include all the names of those who have spoken of the godly qualities they appreciated through knowing Heather, for it would seem that right around the world wherever God used her life to impact others, at whatever level, she became their friend.

Giving our lives totally to Jesus enables each one of to become His friends (John 15:15) and, united in that relationship, friends of each other too. Heather's life so obviously brought a real awareness of that fact to people of every age group, background or nation, leaving a wonderful testimony to the glory of God. But with that testimony, I know Heather would want to leave us a challenge, too, so I want to close this chapter with words given through Dan Sneed at the conclusion of his tribute to her, which I sensed were a particularly anointed message, especially for the next generation; "I can't do this anymore, so I am now handing my baton on to you. Will you take it? Don't let it drop and fall by the wayside. I have invested my life in you. Now it's your turn."

May our response be "Lord, I want to take up Heather's baton and so live my life for you that I too will make a difference, with the one, or many, as I seek to communicate your love and life to people you put along my path—those who you value so much."

*"One loving heart
sets another on fire"*

6

An Anointed Teacher

*It was he [Christ] who gave some to be apostles, some
to be prophets, some to be evangelists, and some to be
pastors and teachers, to prepare God's people for works
of service, so that the body of Christ may be built up
until we all reach unity in the faith and in
the knowledge of the Son of God and become mature,
attaining to the whole measure of the fullness
of Christ.*

Ephesians 4:11-13 NIV

At the Coronation Service of our present Queen,
Elizabeth II, when this young princess very
publicly dedicated her life before God and people
to fulfil the weighty responsibility of becoming Head of
State of our Nation and Commonwealth, a jewel-encrusted
gold crown was placed on her head and a golden orb was
placed in her hands—both symbolizing the rule and
authority that was being bestowed on her. Other symbolic
gifts were also given to her as she made her vows of
dedication to this royal office, but probably the most
significant of them all was the placing of a copy of the Bible
into her hands by the then Archbishop of Canterbury, who

uttered these words; **"This Holy Book—the most valuable thing this world affords."** These words sum up how Heather saw God's Word, for to her it was 'gathered gold' and she never stopped mining into its depths for fresh treasure. And the more God gave her the more she kept on digging, for she knew she had struck pure gold!

Sadly we live in a nation today which has forsaken God's Word and we are seeing the results of this across the whole of society. But I also believe that there is still a deep hunger in the hearts of people to really know God's Truth, because they have been sold a lie. If we go right back to the wonder of God's creation, as recorded in Genesis, we see clearly that man was made in His own image, to know the depth of His amazing love, to live by the truth of His Word and to walk in obedience to His ways, thus enjoying a living relationship with Him. We were made for His pleasure, to be a delight to Him and that deep desire of His heart has not changed, and never will! Our ever-loving Heavenly Father is constantly calling us back to that relationship of 'togetherness' with Him that we might embrace and delight in His Truth. J.I. Packer said, "If I were the devil, one of my first aims would be to stop folk from digging into the Bible." For our enemy knows that the salvation of man is the final purpose of the whole Bible.

Ephesians 4:11 speaks so clearly of the gifts that God has given through Christ so that His body (the people who form His Church), can develop and grow. Praise God, His 'gifts' to the Church are anointed people, not titles and positions. They are 'equippers' whose function it is to prepare its members in such a way that all will be built up in the faith and unity of the knowledge of the Son of God, and in their sharing in the work of ministry together, might become mature.

One thing that was recognized wherever Heather was ministering, in this nation or overseas, was that God's anointing very clearly rested on her as a Bible teacher.

She was gifted and enabled to bring clear interpretation and revelation of God's Word and to help others see how to apply that truth in their daily lives and situations. With this gifting Heather knew the importance of living a life of integrity. One that would in no way conflict with the purity of God's Word, or her own lifestyle, thus discrediting His truth. Her motivation was always her pure love of God's Word, and the passion of her heart was for His people to be so inspired by the Scriptures that they would want to dig for 'gold' themselves.

A legacy of 'gathered gold'

Many people, in paying tribute to Heather, have spoken of the inspiration that Heather's teaching was on a whole range of subjects. Her notebooks are just full of material which was gleaned as she, I would have to say, devoured God's Word and chewed on it until it just became part of her.

She taught on all subjects relating to Marriage and Family:

> *Husbands and Wives; Putting God First in the Family; Motherhood; Fatherhood; Positive Parenthood; Raising and Disciplining Your Children; Family Discipleship; Teenagers; Singleness; Second Marriages; Blended Families and Step Children; Joy in the Family; Single-Parent Families; Becoming a Godly Woman; Romance; Widowhood; Friendship and Joy versus Competition in the Family.*

Added to these are copious notes on Biblical characters such as:

> *Abraham, Jonah, Moses, Samson, David, Mary, Martha, Hannah, Cain and Abel, Caleb, Noah, Zachariah, Isaac, Jacob, Joshua, Joseph and many others.* Plus teaching material on: *The Significance and Power of the Blood of Jesus; Darkness at Noon at*

Christ's Crucifixion; Biblical Feasts; Angels; Total Surrender; Biblical Christians/Cultural Christians; Living as a Victor not a Victim; Knowing and Applying God's Word; Worship; Hindrances to Worship; Handling Pressure; Walking Through Trials; Seasons; Change; Harvest Time; Grief; Deception; Fruitfulness; The Armour of God; Realizing our Full Potential in God; The Promises of God; Making Disciples; Garments; Communication; Covenant; Anointing; The Church; The Passover; Drawing Near; Revival; Prayer; Relationships in the Church; Leadership; The Psalms; Knowing our Destiny; Setting the Captives Free; Clearing Away the Rubbish in our Lives!; Walk, Sit, Stand; The word of our Testimony; Ruth; Sowing and Reaping; Being Kingdom Motivated; Who We Are in Christ; Breaking Down Dividing Walls; Strongholds of the Mind; Abraham's Five Altars; The Importance Of Our words; Fruits of the Holy Spirit; The Importance of Names; Hindrances toSeeing Jesus; Evangelism; Unity; Dealing with Thoughts and Past Failures; Four Priorities for Leadership; Cultural Backgrounds; Passing on our Heritage; Dealing with Emotional Hurts, and An Overview of the Old Testament.

Quite a list, but not an exhaustive one, I would have to say! And added to these notes are, of course, the books she wrote, and those we co-authored together, and the hundreds of Heather's tapes and CDs which are in circulation of her teaching and preaching both here in the UK and around the world. In a nutshell, 'her legacy lives on,' a phrase which has been mentioned so many times as people have paid tribute to Heather.

I have already mentioned Carlyn, the family friend who trained on Team with us and went on to become a vicar. In paying tribute to various aspects of

Heather's life, Carlyn said of her teaching:

"The thing about Heather was that she always taught by example. She was a gifted teacher, not an academic one, but one wise in the Lord. For me her greatest teaching was in how to be a wonderful Christian wife and mother. Whenever I saw her it was as if she had taken the whole of Proverbs 31 from verses 10-29 and digested them in such a way that she naturally lived them out."

That's what I call helpful life-application Bible teaching, and many others share that thought too.

As young Esther Caluzi (soon to become the wife of one of our grandsons) brought greetings from Tanzania at Heather's Thanksgiving Service at our Family Camp at Taunton, Somerset, in August 2007, she spoke of the blessing that Heather was to her family.

She went on to say that, "For most African families, there is a big gap between children and their parents— especially of the father. People say our family is different— there is something so special about your family. They asked my father 'why'? He said 'Everyone says we are a different kind of family. I'll tell you why. It is because I had a 'mother' who took care of me. A mother who taught me how to live and to handle my family. One who showed me how to love and care for my family. That is why we are different'."

Esther talked with people she knew from her own country who had been part of the 'Evangelism Training Course' and found that they all had something good to say about Heather. She spoke of people who recognized her ministry and who had received their own 'call' from God having heard Heather's teachings. She spoke of whole families that had been changed; of new relationships between children and parents. She also talked with the wife of her own pastor in Tanzania who said that she had received a new anointing in her own ministry when Heather prayed for her—a powerful anointing which Esther can recognize every time she preaches now, because she is so different. Praise the Lord! There are others, too, who have received forgiveness, and, as a result, are also learning to forgive.

"Heather's lovely heart was just so pure. You could see within," said Esther. "Just about Heather's heart in coming over to Africa. They pay for everything themselves, and we get the Word of God. That is something that has so touched many in my country.

"Everything that is said about Heather is good, so I have been praying that I will live a life that will touch everyone I meet, too, so that one day when I am gone someone will have something good to say about me."

"What a thought," remarked Alan Penberthy, a dear friend and colleague who was leading that Service, "that when I am gone someone will have something good to say about **me** as they so obviously have about Heather."

You will have already read tributes to Heather from those who were part of our 'extended family' over the years, including cherished memories from David Abbott. During his years in our home, he became so appreciative of the way that Heather taught him to do the most basic things. And for Heather there was no such thing as 'distant learning' it was getting to work on the job in hand **together!** It was seeing Christian responsibility in every aspect of life, and where better to start than in the home, even if that meant decorating or tiling the bathroom! Sadly these days many a young couple starting life together in their own homes don't have a clue about undertaking the responsibilities of some of the most basic practical things, even those coming from Christian families. We need to see a harnessing together of the both the spiritual and the practical so that our homes honour God too.

David said "Heather was the one who helped launch my ministry with children. I was young. At 16, I knew I had a 'call' from God on my life, but Heather was the one who recognized what that 'call' was, and she allowed me to work alongside her and grow as she trained, helped and encouraged me all the way. She was always there for me and never allowed me to struggle, even to the end. She never forced me but encouraged in the background, keeping her motherly eye on me to make sure that everything was OK! And when she moved on to new areas of service herself, she remained a great source of help and advice to me. She had a big heart, which always had room for me!

"On the day Heather was called home I realized that I could have been anywhere in the world with my own Children's ministry, but I was home and was able to see her that afternoon. I did most of the talking because when she took her oxygen mask off she could not breath. But she still found the strength to ask how I was. How my wife Barbara and the children were. How the ministry was going and what our plans were for the future. It was as if she needed to make sure that everything was OK before she went home. Heather was indeed a very special lady, who will always have a special place in my heart," David concluded.

Wanted—spiritual mothers!

In the opening verses of Titus chapter 2 we read of the important ministry of women to women and of the importance of those older in the faith teaching the younger believers to 'love their husbands and children; to be self-controlled and pure; to be busy at home; to be kind;

and to be subject to their own husbands, so that no one would malign the Word of God'. It was from this God-given 'call' that Heather launched the Ladies Conferences, firstly in this nation and then overseas, and they have proved to be so fruitful for all who have been part of them. In fact, I would dare to say, real 'God-encounter' times for everyone!

Paying tribute on behalf of many who have been part of those week-end conferences, Ruth Watkins brought many 'gems' of treasured memories from women she had interviewed about those special times. Many treasured the little personal gifts she made and gave, that were reminders of the themes of those week-ends. Others spoke of the words of Scripture that live in their hearts as treasures of God's Word, and the deep love they felt as Heather conveyed those truths. Her deep joy and happiness, which caused her to laugh a lot, spoke to many others and who could ever forget Heather's special laugh! One of Heather's great loves was that of sheep, and she was able to bring many a Scripture alive as she shared revelation and teaching which the Lord brought her through them; vivid illustrations which live on in the hearts of many of her listeners.

She was recognized as a woman of great strength and integrity; one who was always ready to give a Word in season. The Message speaks of such as one in Proverbs 31, verse 26, in this way *When she speaks she has something worthwhile to say, and she always says it kindly.* Husbands listened as Ruth interviewed various women and she soon realized that whole families had been touched as they not only took Heather's teaching home from those week-end conferences but sought to live it out, for it was more than 'women to women' teaching, it was teaching on how to live godly lives. No wonder this affected the atmosphere of the home and therefore whole families!

As Ruth concluded her tribute to Heather from others,

she added her own precious memories too. Speaking of "one whose wonderful teaching has had a deep impact on my life" she said, "I will personally remember her for that, especially her teaching on the power of the Blood of Jesus. Heather brought so many illustrations that gave such clarity to her teachings and I particularly remember the account of the time when Heather's mother took her to what proved to be a dark and heavy 'meeting' which she discovered was not Christian but 'spiritualist'. Needless to say Heather's mother quickly entered into prayer and as a result the leader of that 'meeting' said 'she was unable to get through because all she could see was a wall of blood.' She recounted so many other stories that were such helpful illustrations of her teachings. Heather was a wonderful woman who impacted so many lives."

Proverbs 31:30 in The Message reads *Charm can mislead and beauty soon fades. The woman to be admired and praised is the woman who lives in the Fear-of-God.* And I would want to add to that—**'that all the glory may go to Him'**.

Dealing with our 'sore spots'

As I have already mentioned, Heather's teachings were not limited to the spoken word but were extended across the world through her writing of a number of books, and tribute was brought through one of her many readers. Mary Price had come to our Family Camp at Taunton recognizing that Heather was anointed as a child of God, a wife, a mother, a grandmother, a leader and a teacher. She recognized her as a beautiful woman of God who had a passion to see people set free; free to enjoy a living relationship with their Father God, and each other. "So why would I need to buy this book of Heather's?" Mary commented. In answer to her own question, she recognized that it was because she had been attracted to the title *Ouch! That Hurt* and the words printed on the cover: *anger, grief, betrayal, criticism, rejection, shame*. Words which so often related to her inner feelings. Mary went on to say that, "I was saved, healed, forgiven, empowered by the Holy Spirit, but so often I got frustrated with things, situations and even people! Something would happen and then 'bang'! Why? Because I had some sore spots of anger and hurt, and I could identify with the title of the book."

Ouch! That Hurt looks at different Biblical heroes such as Samson, Hannah, David, Moses and others who reacted in real life situations, often with tragic consequences, because of their own unresolved hurts. And it can be the same for us if we don't deal with those hidden 'time bombs'. How we respond to hurt determines whether our spirits will grow and blossom, or wither and die. As Heather's husband, I can testify that the revelation God gave her, which is the message of this book, was life-changing to Heather and it contains both her own testimony of how God had brought her through into freedom, and a Biblically-based solution for others to follow in order to find their own release in Him.

Mary concluded her tribute to Heather with a quote from the final chapter of *Ouch! That Hurt*:

"There is only one thing left and that is for you to apply what you have read so that you can be free from emotional hurt of any kind. It is not essential for you to have a deliverance session, nor is there a need for you to go to any special person or place. In your own time, in your own home, you can apply what Jesus has done. You can receive what He has purchased for you on the Cross into your own life. How can you do this? By coming to the foot of the Cross, and acknowledging that you are hurt."

Living Free

Heather had a deep desire to continually live in God's grace, so she was always keen to turn to God's Word and search the Scriptures for His answers to her own needs.

You know, we can so easily miss the grace of God and end up living in our own prisons far longer than we need to, because we fail to lay hold of that amazing gift of God that is ours to receive through Christ. The teachings of Heather's book show us not only the way to know God's freedom through His grace, but how to continue to live free. It has proved to be one that contains a life-changing message which He has used to bring countless people into freedom, and as I write it is being translated into other languages for use around the world, especially in the African countries.

Gill Gifford, who herself is in ministry and has served with us in various capacities over the years, wrote this testimony in tribute to Heather:

"Almost thirty years ago, when I first met Heather, I knew that the Lord had placed a very godly woman in my life. I loved her, and I loved her teaching, and I was inspired by her grasp of Scripture. But most of all I could see that she was a woman who lived the Word, especially in her example as wife and mother, and this challenged every facet of my life! Like me, I am sure that Heather brought hope and encouragement to many to press on even when there seemed to be no way.

"I clearly remember her brilliant teaching about being redeemed from the curse and reading her book 'Twentieth Century Eve' over and over again. Heather always had the capacity to communicate personally to her readers, and God used that book to plant faith in me to believe for a symptom-free menopause! 'Of course you can!' was Heather's reply when I enquired if that was really possible for me. She truly believed that nothing was impossible in Christ. I am eternally grateful that this has been my testimony—to the glory of God.

"As the years passed, I was privileged to get to know Heather personally as a very precious friend who always spoke deeply into my life. She has left me, and thousands of other women, I am sure, with an everlasting legacy."

Another area of ministry where Heather's teaching has been so appreciated is through our Marriage Seminars; in this nation and overseas. Bringing their own tribute at Heather's Thanksgiving Service on behalf of others who have also been part of those teaching times, Andrew and Michelle Duff recalled:

"We first met Don and Heather as a young couple with our first baby. Life seemed great, and yet we knew we need something more! We are talking now of 30 years ago, when we had heard about the GNC Camps at Blaithwaite—so we went.

"The lasting memory of Don and Heather during that time was how much they enjoyed each other. We were so self-centred! That week God spoke to us and we knew He was showing us to put Him first in our marriage. Don and Heather were so much part of this revelation—**Christ in the centre**—and with Him in that place we would become closer to each other. We had begun to realize what it really was for two to become one in Him, and our marriage has never been the same since! We saw something of the quality and reality of Don and Heather's own marriage. We saw their sense of romance and fun, both together and in their family, and it spoke to us.

"Heather has always been an inspiring model to us. She was a great teacher who was able to explain things so clearly and give you the tools to do the job yourselves. She was such a blessing and we know that her ministry has helped so many other couples around this nation and overseas, as well as wives and mothers.

"Both Don and Heather have been key influences in our lives, and their teaching will stay with us for the rest of our live, especially in the area of marriage. They have given us new vision for how God intended marriage. We have seen how every marriage is a microcosm of Church and His Kingdom and the need to 'model' that to others. Of having a home for God which displays fun, togetherness and a different quality of life. They encouraged us, too, to have an 'open home' for God to us, with all its risks! Since then we have had some interesting people in our home, but we don't blame Don and Heather for that!

"The 'extended family' that Don and Heather welcomed as their own and the amazing mother and 'spiritual mother' that Heather was, have all spoken so much to us as a couple. But not only to us but also to our family, so that teaching is already influencing the next generation.

"Both Don and Heather have helped us to have new direction and new hope for the renewal of marriages that is real and lasting, and we are now involved in marriage 'mentoring' ourselves. The input that Heather had as she ministered into our lives is now being multiplied around the country, and indeed around the world as that vision is passed on to many more, and we praise God that the legacy she left lives on."

'A legacy to be passed on' was indeed the desire of Heather's heart throughout her life and ministry, for she saw the revelation that God had brought to her as a gift to be shared, and thus multiplied through the hands of the Giver, for His glory alone.

- 7 -

A Prepared Missionary

Then I heard the voice of the Lord saying,
"Whom shall I send? And who will go for us?
And I said "Here am I. Send me!"
Isaiah 6: 8

Then Jesus came to them and said
"All authority in heaven and on earth has
been given to me.
Therefore go and make disciples of all
nations, baptizing them in the name of the
Father and of the Son and of the Holy Spirit,
and teaching them to obey everything I have
commanded you. And surely I am with you
always, to the very end of the age"
Matthew 28: 19

From the time that Heather became a Christian, filled with the life and power of the Holy Spirit, she became a true worshipper, for she had a heart that desired above everything to see God, to hear His voice and to be obedient to His Will for her life. And it was from that place of intimacy, of knowing that she was seated with Him in Heavenly places (which is so beautifully pictured for us in Ephesians 2:6), that Heather saw worship as the very essence of her life. So often people talk of worship as something that we 'do', but rather it is a God-given relationship for us to enjoy as we realize the purpose for which He created us. It is only in that place that we are changed from one degree of glory to another as we behold His glory through our adoration and contemplation of Him in all His awesome splendour.

It was William Temple who once said, "Worship is the submission of all our nature to God. It is the quickening of our conscience by **His holiness**; the nourishment of our mind with **His Truth**; the purifying of our imagination by **His beauty**; the opening of our heart to **His love**; and the surrender of our will to **His purpose**." What a different picture this gives us of worship, of transcendent wonder. I believe that it was from this place, of sharing that *joint seating* with Him in those Heavenly places (as the Amplified Bible says), that Heather was able to so clearly hear the voice of God, know His anointing, and live right in the centre of His will, whether that be as a homemaker, friend, helper, teacher, missionary or whatever, knowing her 'calling' from Him; that appointing and equipping for the task.

Heather's heart was set on 'pilgrimage' and when, like Isaiah, she heard Father, Son and Holy Spirit sharing a need for someone to undertake a particular task and pondering "who will go for Us", she was ready and willing to also respond "here am I, send me." How different that task becomes when it is born out of such a response, rather than our own strivings or ambitions.

Among Heather's treasured notes are many 'prophetic' words which were given to her and myself over the years, words which spoke so clearly of the 'wider ministry' that the Lord was going to open up to us as individuals and together. Something new was being birthed in our hearts, but we had learned that God's Word instructs us to 'weigh' those things carefully, even if brought through trusted people. While He calls for our instant obedience, I believe that this is more a matter of embracing it in our hearts straight away rather than always of jumping into immediate action, particularly when He is bringing new direction. Many people have ended up moving out of His will and purposes by acting prematurely.

But the Lord was clearly confirming both His direction and timing to us and we knew that we could step confidently through those doors which He was opening up to us. For Heather this meant being released to travel more into wider ministry, both with me and as an individual. She had known the importance of heeding the last words of Jesus Himself, before He was taken up into Heaven, to be His witness in her own *Jerusalem*, and now it seemed that (metaphorically) *all Judea and Samaria, and the ends of the earth* were being opened up to her too! She had learned whilst at home to buy up every opportunity she had to sit at Jesus' feet and learn of Him and, therefore, the shelves of the 'store cupboards' of her heart were filled with 'treasure' imparted from His Word. Treasure which could help new Christians and those with hungry hearts for God to grow in their understanding of Him and His Truth, for it was both revealed Truth and proven Truth. And so it was that we saw the beginning of a greater ministry than we had ever seen before.

A prophetic word brought through Dan Sneed spoke of 'God bringing a fresh release of the Holy Spirit to Heather which would bring her into the flow of what He wanted to do through her life as one who had already emerged as a strong woman of God. As the Lord continued His deep work in Heather's heart so her thinking would be revolutionized and He would move her into new dimensions of ministry and service, and she would become even stronger in His new flow and anointing than she had ever experienced before.'

Many other such words were given, specifically relating to a fresh anointing to teach others, which just confirmed God's unfolding plans for Heather's life and so naturally took her into realms of His supernatural gifting; and her teaching became more and more sought after and appreciated wherever God directed her paths. At the celebration event for our 25th Wedding Anniversary the late Dr. Judson Cornwall, a friend and well-loved Camp and international Conference speaker, brought this prophetic word to us which we documented. It reads:

"Your previous years together have built faith and confidence in God, but behold the Lord will do a new thing —a fresh new thing in you. And because of that new thing **in** you He will do a fresh new thing **through** you. Your youth will be renewed as the eagles; your strength will be restored on a day by day basis; your faith in God will reach to greater heights than you have ever known, and the areas of your ministry will expand beyond the borders that you've ever been used in. For God has chosen you for something very real and special in the coming revival that will sweep this world and His Name shall be great in the two of you. For as you have poured yourself into others, their ministries shall flow out in many directions as a river branches out into streams. You will be renewed, refreshed, strengthened and enlarged and God will do mighty things **through** you, and He will challenge you to keep humble and pure and to walk gently before Him in the days before you—as you have in the days behind you. For you are no more capable of facing the future than you were capable of facing the past, but He who has brought you this far is faithful and will lead you step by step as the Father leads a child. He will put into your mouth the words to be spoken, and into your hands the power to be released, for God will be mighty within you."

Heather was not one for labels. She just saw herself as an obedient follower of the Lord Jesus, a costly path maybe, but knowing that it costs more not to follow Him, for finding yourself on a path without Him is a risky place to be. And so it was that she just kept walking and each new step seemed to open up a new vista of opportunity to share those revealed treasures of the Truth of His Word that He had put in her heart.

Feeding the hungry!

The birth of the 'Evangelist Training Course' in 1996 (with its ten weeks of intensive residential training, then sending them back to their localities called of God and equipped to put into practice everything they have been trained for), was something which was welcomed by students of all ages in this country and overseas. Although the training base for this has now moved from the UK to Kenya, it continues to be a much-sought after resource for teaching those with a heart for evangelism and ministry, and the fruitfulness of those we have trained through this Course has proved to be one of the most encouraging aspects of our ministry for more than a decade.

Among the first 'students' in the UK were Don and Anne Trahearn who benefited enormously from their training with us. They were already established 'evangelists' out on the job, so to speak, but their time on the ETC Course seemed to ignite a fresh flame in their hearts for the Gospel, as well as a new anointing in ministry. Anne has already mentioned what an affect Heather had on her life through those well-remembered words of hers "course you can" but they remain a significant truth to her, and many others, as they continue to move out in new faith steps in God. Heather's encouragement and challenge has caused many an intrepid pioneer to move out into new territory in the power of the Holy Spirit. Don and Anne look back on 'active service' with us through mission trips to India, Kenya, Tanzania, Zanzibar, the Seychelles, Poland (as well as various parts of the UK) and on many other visits they have since made to these places for follow-up and as their own growing ministries have developed. In addition they have led tours to Israel on our behalf and spear-headed their own missions in other places. What a privilege it is to be able to impart to others what the Lord has invested in your own life and to see them sharpened up to function in their own giftings too.

Don and Anne were always amazed by Heather's knowledge of each country that we visited together on mission trips, and appreciated the way she was able to impart this in an informative and lively way. Her great love of Israel and its history is something which many people have commented on, for Heather was able to present these with both enthusiasm and accuracy causing Scriptural references to events, places and even parables, to come alive to eager listeners. Life was never dull around Heather for she always had something of worth to contribute in her own endearing way.

Ron and Liz Bignell were also part of our ETC Course. Again more mature 'students' who already had a heart for evangelism, but who sought to dig deeper in Him in order to become stronger in every area of life and ministry. In recalling that time, and subsequent mission trips that they shared with us, they speak of:

"Heather's sound teaching of the Word of God, and of the succinct way she was able to present it. She had a great ability in identifying the key points in the questions asked, or the lack of understanding expressed by the 'students', and was always able to respond with clarity and help — and often with a great sense of humour too, which the students loved. The great thing was that those attributes featured consistently in Heather's life and ministry —

whether on mission, at Camp or at other events. Heather was a great encourager to all of us, as well as an outstanding model of a godly, yet very practical, wife and mother."

Someone else who trained with us through the 'Evangelism Training Course' was Richard Trotter. Richard too, who has served with us in many places, came on a mission we ran in Broughton, Cumbria. Writing of one of his fond memories of that time he says:

"As part of the mission team, I arrived at the local village hall one evening, together with my son James, who was then nineteen years of age. There were only a handful of people there at the time and as I looked around before the meeting I saw James and Heather sitting together in the middle of the hall in deep conversation with each other. It always amazed me that Heather, being a wife, mother and grandmother, as well as having a busy schedule, had time for people, no matter what their age. For there was this young man, who came to his first GNC Camp at nine months of age, talking with this woman of God who, over the subsequent years, had influenced his life a lot through her teachings and inspiration. The memory of this aspect of Heather 'on mission' and her personal encouragement to James really blesses me every time I think of her."

We travelled together and apart to many countries, as you know, but Heather had a huge heart for the African nations. So much so that you should have seen the mail I received following her 'home call'. I guess it also showed me what a huge heart those people had for Heather too. The Africans absolutely loved her teaching, especially from the Old Testament. In fact they were 'over the moon', as the saying goes—especially by her knowledge of Israel and its history. I often think of the training Heather was able to pass on to others who attended the various conferences and training events we held over the years, as well as to the students of the ETC Courses as 'life-giving seed', and it thrills me to think of the seeds of her teaching still bearing fruit as they are being passed on around the world—a multiplication process which can reach multi-thousands with the powerful truths of the Gospel. What a legacy!

Rwanda always had a special place in Heather's heart (in fact this is true for both of us) and the relationship we shared with Gilbert Habimana, and his beloved wife Odette, has been a very important part of that. Rwanda is a very beautiful country and we ministered there a lot over the years. They really loved Heather's ministry and we saw the Lord do some amazing things during our visits there, especially in the midst of crises. At one of our Crusades in the Olympic Stadium a large percentage of the vast crowd were soldiers in their uniforms. On this occasion we were restricted to the capital because of the war being fought in the rural areas. It was an amazing experience seeing many of them responding to the call of the Gospel and getting saved and healed.

Throughout the genocide we continued to support Gilbert, his family and their ministry there. During this time they were in the Refugee Camp but they continued with their ministry of leadership, prayer and fasting with other believers, which enabled him to play a major part in taking the people back to Rwanda, something which amazed the world! Heather and I always considered it such a privilege to be in relationship with such a guy, who always came to spend time with us whenever we were in East Africa.

Then came Heather's book *Ouch! That Hurt* which was translated into the Kinyarwandan language. God is still using this in amazing ways to bring healing to many traumatized teenagers who saw families slaughtered in the genocide, and in a recent letter from Rwanda giving news and up-date (which is always good to hear), I was also thrilled to read the following extract: "Testimonies are still coming from those who read *Ouch! That Hurt* and who have experienced a new transformation. This could be something which will help more students and young people in the future."

Joan from Nairobi writes: "Since my training at Eldoret I have seen my life change. I am doing crusades in local towns around Nairobi and people are giving their lives to Jesus." Emmanuel from Tanzania writes: "I was one of the students in 2003. Heather's teachings shaped my life. I was a man of low self-esteem with no hope for the future. What I learned from her teachings and her book *Ouch! That Hurt* brought God's healing to my emotional wounds". John, another student from Tanzania, writes: "I am doing well with my Church and prison ministry. God is using me in a new dimension. Many prisoners are being saved." Many other ETC students shared their sadness at receiving the news of Heather's passing as they loved and appreciated her so much. For Dan from Kenya, he spoke of this news as a "great grief. I can remember when she spoke in the college (ETC) on how to deal with emotional hurt. This message turned my life completely. I want to let all of you know that I had a wonderful trip to Somalia and six people gave their lives whilst we were there."

Heather would never have seen herself as an 'evangelist' as she saw this as the anointing that God has given me, but she nevertheless had a big heart for people to come to know the Lord Jesus Christ personally. I guess we always made a good team though, inasmuch as our specific anointed ministries complemented each others. How wonderfully God matched up our lives to bring together not only two lives that could live in His harmony and blessing, but that could be effective fruit-bearers in His

Kingdom purposes. But didn't He say in John 15 that in His plan He chose us as His 'friends' to do just that!

And these signs shall accompany those who believe . . .

Over the years in our ministry overseas we received many letters of testimony from people that God had touched (perhaps more numerous in number than could possibly be recorded through the pages of this book), but I was delighted to find among Heather's 'treasures' recently a little booklet in which she had written some of these testimonies. She recalled how one day early on in our ministry (more than 40 years ago) we were feeling rather low. We had no money and things seemed really tough. Receiving mail has always been a great encouragement to us and it is a very welcome blessing at such times, isn't it. We normally receive lots of correspondence from people all around the world who write to us telling us how the Lord has blessed them through various missions, camp meetings, conferences, books we have written, or whatever, but this particular day we had only one letter, with a post mark from Nigeria. To our shame we were tempted not to open it, thinking it might be asking for some financial help that we knew we were not in a position to give at that time, and we were just feeling too down to open it. However, we decided to open it anyway and how wrong we were! For out of it fell a £1 note which was of much more value then than it is today, and it had come all the way from Nigeria. How our spirits soared! If God could prompt someone in Africa to send us £1 and for them to be obedient enough to post it all the way to England, just at the right time for us to receive it on that very day when we most needed it, but more especially the encouragement it brought, then we knew that God wasn't through with us yet and that He would always provide, just as He had promised. Needless to say, we repented, picked ourselves up off the floor, brushed ourselves down and we were ready to go again, with renewed fervour. God is good **all** the time!

Another time we were in Kenya where we met a man who had been in prison for robbery for 18 months. On his release he saw the posters for a Crusade we were holding and apparently thought, "I'll go and steal something to sell to get some money for food," so he came with that intention. However, the moment he got onto the site all he could say was "I'm a thief. I need JESUS." The Crusade security guards were faced with a situation that they did not know how to handle, thinking, 'Do we take him to the police or what?' They took the decision to wait until the morning when the local Church 'day watchmen' were due to come, so he slept the night with the security guards. Next morning, at the appropriate time, they handed him over to the 'day watchmen', as planned, but instead of them handing him on to the police, they led Him to the Lord (Hallelujah!) and he then went to the morning 'follow-up' meeting, where again God touched his life and he was filled with the Holy Spirit!

Another time back in this country we needed to travel by car to fulfil some planned ministry but we had no money. "What do we do?" we thought. "Do we say we can't go, or do we trust God?" Being those who were seeking to trust God totally along this new path of faith, we decided to trust Him! So we drove into a garage and started to fill up the car with petrol. We had absolutely no idea how we would be able to pay for it, but believed God had said. "Trust Me." It is far easier to do that when the provision is already there, isn't it, rather than to be in an 'eleventh hour and fifty-nine minute' situation, like we were in, when the Enemy seeks to sow doubts like 'Now what are you going to do?' into your hearts. Thankfully we were able to make the choice to agree with God and just then another car came into the garage, the driver got out, came across the forecourt and said "I'll pay for your petrol," and he did! We knew this man only by sight and he lived in Cornwall, but we were in a garage in Northampton! Some might say that was a sheer coincidence, but we knew it was our ever-faithful Heavenly Father keeping His promises to us in a miraculous way as we trusted Him.

On one occasion we were in Kampala in Uganda conducting two days of Married Couples' Seminars, with 900 local Pastors, Ministers and with top business people present. In those situations it is so easy to be fearful of culture, but you know Biblical principles are the same the world over, and we need to present His Word with that assurance because people are hungry for Truth. As we did just that, without compromise, they requested that we go back. They wanted more because never before had they had such straight Bible teaching on marriage. In their culture it was normal for the wife to be seen as a 'slave' to serve the husband, but instead we taught from Ephesians 5:25 on the importance of 'husbands *loving* their wives as Christ loved the Church'. At the end of the week we saw such a transformation as husbands were responding to the Lord and taking hold of the hand of their wife. Only the Word of God has power to break through cultural practices and bring people into freedom in Christ.

Kenya, as we all know, has been in the throes of political upheaval in recent times bringing much heartache, suffering and even killing to people that hold a special place in our hearts, but how I thank the Lord that we have been privileged to share the Gospel and minister there together over the years. It has been impressed on my heart how important it is to be obedient to the Lord and to 'go' whenever and wherever He appoints us as He opens up those opportunities. Praise God, despite the trouble in that land, miraculously the classroom that we are building in Eldoret in memory of Heather has still continued to be built.

Two dear friends in that country, Godfrey and Elisabeth Dawkins, who minister in Nairobi, paid tribute to Heather in this way.

"It is always good to be able to say something good about one of God's dear children, as Heather was. But actually what we want to say is more about what we didn't see than what we saw! We did not see Heather in person for many years because she stayed at home in England looking after the children while Don was away on evangelistic tours, including his many missionary journeys to Africa. That meant two things. One, as a wife Heather unselfishly released Don from any domestic chores and supported him whole-heartedly to obey his God-given call to fulfil the Great Commission. Here we saw Heather's 'first love' for the Lord Jesus and her unstinting obedience to His call; no doubt at great personal cost. And two, as a mother she was always there for her children in their formative years and could never be accused of having attended to ministry matters at their expense. Moreover, she was there for them — and other people's children as well, like one little girl we knew of personally who found refuge in their home for several years. We want to add our 'thank you' to those of the Lord for her faithful obedience.

"But with the children grown up and flown from the nest, Heather knew she was able to travel with Don, and this was the time when we saw her in action and came to know and love her in person. Coming in and out of the country, whether for Schools of Evangelism or Crusades, we would welcome Don and Heather as our house guests. Sometimes it would be at the commencement of their tour when they were 'bright-eyed and bushy-tailed' and rearing to go, and at other times it would be on their way out when they were feeling exhausted. Heather particularly loved wildlife, so it was good at such times to be able to have the opportunity of taking them on outings such as to the Giraffe Centre. Always a favourite!

"Whether in season or out of season Don and Heather always maintained a regime of strict discipline, praying and reading God's Word together in their room. Or sometimes Heather would be writing another book, or taking dictation for another of Don's books, in the loggia overlooking the garden.

"The students loved Heather's ministry. There was one student whom I had sent to them whose 'call' was in question. It seemed nobody else believed in him, except me! Yet Don and Heather came alongside financially and help me pick him up and put him on his feet. It was that Christ-like, kindred spirit of theirs in 'not breaking a bruised reed or quenching the smoking flax' that I found especially endearing. We honour Heather as a highly effective woman of God."

In our ministry together in Kenya we saw many miracles as God confirmed His Word with signs and wonders following. A man who hadn't been able to walk for ten years because of swollen joints was healed. Another man who was crippled and had not been able to touch his feet for twenty years was freed. We saw a little girl completely healed who had previously not been able to walk for ten years. A lady who had tumours growing under her arms was healed as the tumours disappeared. A dumb girl spoke. We saw another lady healed who had previously had stomach trouble for seventeen years. God touched another lady who had not been able to bend her knees for a number of years and she was able to kneel. It was very moving to see another little 18-month old boy whose legs had been so affected by polio that he couldn't stand. After prayer he stood on the platform alongside his mother. We saw hair grow back on another lady's head who had previously lost all her hair. These are just a few of the miracles we documented from our ministry there, for which all the glory belongs to our ever-loving and all-powerful God.

From Singida Tanzania I received this tribute. "I knew Heather well and she was a 'Mama of ministry' in all her life. She was a great blessing to us in many things— especially her ladies seminars here in Singida, and as an author of many books containing teaching on the Word of God. One of those which she left as a gift to us was the one entitled *Ouch That Hurt!* This book is a real treasure for everyone who reads it. Heather was a remarkable lady with a remarkable ministry because she was on fire for Jesus!"

Heather didn't know of any other way to be, than passionate in her faith in God and ablaze for Him. Turning to Romans 12 we read of the *voluntary spiritual act of our worship* that God desires of us in *presenting our bodies to Him as a living sacrifice on His altar. No longer conformed to the pattern of this world but transformed by the renewing of our mind.* Of being *totally surrendered to Him and His purposes so that we can prove what is will is, His good, pleasing and perfect will.* What a fitting description of the will of God is described in these three words; good, pleasing and perfect. It's like stepping into a suitable and comfortable pair of shoes for the journey ahead of walking with Him!

Heather sought only to be in the centre of God's will, wherever God had planned for that to be, so she was a role model to all she met of one surrendered to Him. I guess we all have role models if we are honest. Those who live godly lives that we want to emulate. For Timothy it was Paul. They had lived and worked alongside each other in the various terrains of life's journey. They knew each other well and young Timothy saw something in Paul that he wanted to follow. We only have to read Paul's words of challenge and encouragement in 2 Timothy 3: 10-17 to realize that he was in no way bragging when he reminds

Timothy of his own life. Rather he is encouraging him to live a consistent life in a hostile world, consistent in what he believed, how he behaved, and in what his life's aim was, for he wanted young Timothy to go on following his example after he had died so that he, too, would be a role model to others. The secret of Paul's consistency amid so much moral decline, empty religion and false teaching was, of course, because he was following a greater role-model! In 1 Corinthians 1:11, 1 Thessalonians 1:6 and Philippians 3:17 Paul specifically mentions that he himself had made the Lord Jesus Christ his role model, and this, I believe, was why so many people around the world sought to follow Him through Heather's life example too.

No longer my own—but Yours!

Heather's early days in the Methodist Church saw her taking part in the prayer of the 'Covenant Service' which was traditionally held on the first Sunday of each New Year. This prayer is one of thanksgiving to God for the year that had passed, and of commitment for the new year ahead, the words of which include: "I am no longer my own, but Yours. Put me to what You will; rank me with whom You will; put me to doing, put me to suffering; let me be employed for You or laid aside for You, exalted or brought low for You; let me be full, let me be empty; let me have all things, let me have nothing; I freely and whole-heartedly yield all things to Your pleasure and disposal". Heather no doubt prayed this prayer many times in her endeavour to be totally surrendered to the Lord, thus pointing her own followers to her own life model, the Lord Jesus Christ.

One the places Heather and I ministered many times was Uganda and, as you may recall, Heather had a big heart to see the development of a particularly derelict site transformed into school classrooms and a playground area for the children. It was a vision which, thanks to the generosity of those who shared this vision with us, we were able to see fulfilled. As Daniel Nkata, of *Reach-out Ministries*, recounts our time together there, he writes:

"I am grateful for the opportunity of writing about remarkable Mamma Heather. To us she was everything you can think about. We worked with her very closely from 1987 and she influenced us in so many ways. To my wife, Margaret, she was like her elder sister, and the last time we were together in Mubende we saw achievements in our calling to ministry. When she arrived we did not know it would be the last time we would be with her. Heather encouraged us to always look to God who called and chose us for his service.

"She was a great teacher with a lot of concern for her class. In the last training in Kenya they put me in the same room with the students, which was alright for me but I decided to pay for myself in an Eldoret Hotel. When Don and Heather learned about this, Heather insisted that I should not spend money in a hotel, and she invited me to join them in the house where they were staying. This was a great honour for me as it has always been my desire to be closer to the people God is using to affect many people's lives.

"Mamma and Papa Double have been the source of great learning to us at *Reach-out Ministries*. The level of their humbleness and transparency in their work have given us a good challenge to also be honest in our ministry. Mamma Heather was always very frank on finances and I learned that if she was convinced, Papa Double wouldn't say no! We are very grateful to Mamma Heather for helping us to create opportunities for our poor children to have classrooms and a playground—a vision which was initiated by Mamma Heather and approved and sponsored by *Good News Crusade* and the *Double family*.

"When we were in Tanzania she was very committed to

teach me how to use my telephone to send messages, and by the time I left I had managed to do so. It is a great loss for Mamma Heather to depart, but we know that she lived as a testimony and she has only changed her address to a better one!"

Wherever she went around the world Heather seemed to be able to reach out across all age barriers and encourage those who she recognised as 'treasure seekers', those whose hearts were wanting to chase *righteousness, godliness, faith, love, endurance and gentleness* (1 Timothy 6:11), through a closer and deeper relationship with God. Brother Lazaro Mahewa, a former ETC student from Singida, writes:

"It is marvellous to speak of Heather's ministry for she went around the world with Don teaching the Word of God in deep consideration. She was a 'mother of mothers' among the ladies of the Church.

"Heather knew how to deal with difficult spiritual issues among the believers. I once tried to ask her some questions about the women in the Church who don't like to get married She answered me in an unexpected and wonderful way, for she knew how to deal with the problems of emotional hurt, a big disease in the people of God. Heather was a Bible teacher and her teachings were prophetic messages toward her listeners—messages which will not be forgotten.

"She was a careful driver on the roads too and therefore was a good driver for Don's evangelism trips as she drove with consideration in all situations."

How important these practical aspects of a person's life and witness are, for reckless driving can be a real contradiction to our testimony and witness.

It has been a real thrill to me to read the many tributes

that have been paid to Heather from around the world and to see the how God has used the various aspects of her life and ministry to touch the lives of others. Our dear friends Alf and Hilary Cooper, in Chile, in paying tribute to Heather write:

"We remember Heather as Don's perfect complement. They would come out to Chile together and Heather would always be the master planner and organizer. I have memories of picking them up from their simple hotel bedrooms where we would find Heather scurrying about packing suitcases, whilst Don was lying on the bed with his Bible preparing the next message. He would shout 'Hallelujah!' and Heather would reply 'Amen!' and carry on packing! She would often have the latest *Palm Top* or *Psion*, as she was a very orderly person, and we would get engrossed in chatting about the benefits of these. Her persuasiveness usually resulted in me getting one.

"Whenever Heather or Don got up to preach, in the most unlikely cultural settings among the Mapuche Indians to the Santiago shanty towns, somehow their message was always culturally relevant. They truly spoke the message of the Kingdom taught by the Holy Spirit. Heather moved mightily in faith, in prophecy and in words of wisdom, and yet it was all tempered with a practical, motherly tenderness and firmness that brought home the message.

"Heather was a spiritual 'Mum' to us all in Chile, wherever she passed through. While Don thundered his faith message home she would back him totally, as well as preaching her own brand of 'fire' to wives and mothers; teaching them how 'the hand that rocks the cradle moves the world'. I can still remember translating her Cornish into Spanish, wit and all! We so loved Heather and remember her with much affection and gratitude."

Another of the places which the Lord opened up to us was India, and Heather grew to really love the people there. We ministered in India twice, in 1995 and again in 1998, at 'Good News Festivals' in Trivandrum and Tiruvalla. Writing of the time that Heather spent there, Pappy Daniel writes:

"She had such a love and compassion for our people that she even found time to go to the slum areas where people lived in demonic oppression, poverty and disease. People were so impressed with her radiant shining face and the love of Jesus was so evident in her powerful words. The believers in those areas were strengthened in faith and many came to know the Lord Jesus for the first time.

"Her ministry among women and children was instrumental in immense blessings for many. There were a number of healings from asthmatic conditions, arthritis, bodily pain, ulcers, hearing and eye problems and others were delivered from satanic bondages. Heather's ministry to our orphaned children was also of great blessing, a number of them dedicating their lives for the Lord's work as she served among them. One of the girls, named Renjitha, is now attending a seminary towards a Bachelor of Divinity degree, after securing a degree in Mathematics with high honours."

Heather's clear anointing was that of a Bible teacher and one who disciples, so what motivated her was to see people build their lives on what God says in His Word, with the clear goal of producing disciples who are one hundred per cent followers of Jesus. And from all around the world have come words of appreciation from people of all ages who have developed a real hunger for God and His Word through both Heather's life and her teaching. Lives that have been eternally changed, who simply say, "We thank God for every remembrance of Heather. What a great joy it will be to see her again one day in Glory!"

Yes, and what a re-union that time will be as we meet those who we have had the privilege of serving with or ministering to; dear saints of God from all around the world gathering together to worship Him around the Throne for all of eternity. When the ministry gifts He graciously gave us won't matter any more and the only important thing, as Heather has already realized, will be that 'our names too are enrolled in Heaven'.

> *However, we possess this precious treasure*
> *[the divine Light of the Gospel]*
> *in [frail, human] vessels of earth,*
> *that the grandeur and exceeding greatness*
> *of the power may be shown to be from God*
> *and not from ourselves.*
> 2 Corinthians 4: 7 Amplified Bible

And to HIM be all the glory!

- 8 -

Just Heather

"Be still, and know that I am God."
Psalm 46:10

Arise, my love, my fair one and come away.
[So I went with him, and when we were climbing the rocky
steps up the hillside, my beloved shepherd said to me]
O my dove, [while you are here] in the seclusion of
the clefts in the solid rock, in the sheltered and secret place of
the cliff, let me see your face, let me hear your voice;
for your voice is sweet, and your face is lovely.
Song of Songs 2:13b-14 AMP

It is said that "we are what we are when we are alone
with God"—a phrase which is probably not the best of
English grammar, but one which, nonetheless, in the
clumsiness of its words, expresses something which is so
true. For it is only as we draw close to the Lord that we find
our true selves and discover the intimate relationship
which He longs to share with us. It is wonderful to be in a
good Church, have good leadership, hear anointed
speakers and to be encouraged and helped by others in our
walk with God. All those aspects are great, but the reality

is that no one else can actually walk that walk *for* us. No one else, however close they are to us, can have a deep personal relationship with God for us. It has to be our own.

Heather lived to know and experience that deep intimate relationship with the One who had changed her life. From the time that she first met Jesus as her own Lord and Saviour as a young child, a deep longing was birthed in her heart and spirit to be more *intimately acquainted with Him*—as the Amplified Bible so beautifully puts it. The Psalmist describes that longing in Psalm 42 in this way, *As the hart* [deer] *pants and longs for the water brooks, so I pant and long for You, O God. My inner self thirsts for God, for the Living God.* It is an amazing paradox, isn't it, that Jesus totally satisfies us. Yet the more we drink of the life-giving water of His Spirit the more thirsty we become, and the more we feed on Him, the Bread of Life, the more hungry we become, because He is the God of the 'so much more!'

Heather made no secret of the fact that she was hungry and thirsty for Him. Her heart-cry was for more of Him and her soul yearned to dwell in His presence as she lived out her life for Him day by day. She had entered into that 'divine romance' and she knew that it was not just her seeking Jesus, the lover of her soul, but that He was seeking her! How different our lives become when we have the revelation of that concept.

Heather knew a total dependence on God, and, therefore, she was desperate for Him. Desperate to be closer to Him and to know more of His reality in her life. We read in Scripture of John the disciple who showed that longing, too, as he laid his head on Jesus' breast. Jesus was within touching distance of him and yet John's desperation drove him to an act that made others react, probably out of jealousy. But he did not care what others thought or said, he just wanted to get closer.

Mary, too, dared to interrupt the agenda of others when she anointed Jesus' feet with her precious ointment, and her tears! This act of deep devotion, resulting in the whole house being filled with the fragrance of her love, so blessed Jesus that he said *"Wherever this Gospel is preached throughout the world, what she has also done will be told, in memory of her."* (Matthew 26:13) Her gift was one of extravagance where intimacy overruled intellect: and her passion, her desperation, over-ruled logic. Perhaps we have been in that place, too, with our children as parents or grandparents, when the extravagance of our love for them went far beyond what we could naturally afford, but we were desperate to express our appreciation of them.

Moses said, "Show me your glory, Lord." He was not satisfied with what he had. He, too, wanted more.

This was Heather's heart. She desired to respond to His invitation, recorded in Isaiah 55: 1-3, *"**Come**—all you who are thirsty, come to the waters; and you who have no money, come, buy and eat! Come, buy wine and milk without money and without cost. Why spend money on what is not bread, and your labour on what does not satisfy? **Listen**, listen to Me, and **eat** what is good, and your soul will **delight** in the richest of fare. Give ear and come to me; hear me, that your soul may **live**."*

I guess if we were to select a Biblical character who influenced Heather's life greatly, most of us would chose Abraham, for whenever she shared there was very often a reference to his life and walk of faith woven in somewhere. I often picture her actually meeting up with him in Heaven and finding out even more about him! As I have said many times already, Heather was a worshipper in all its different facets. She loved to draw close to the Lord and give expression of those love songs in her heart for Him. She loved to worship Him, too, through serving, helping, caring, encouraging, teaching. In fact, she rightly saw her whole life as worship, knowing that every activity can be transformed into an act of worship when it is done for the praise, glory and pleasure of God.

One of the passages which really spoke to Heather a

lot was in Genesis 12, where we read of the call of Abram (before his name was changed to Abraham). As a result of God speaking to him about leaving his own country, his family and his people, at seventy-five years old, he set out, with the promises that God had given him, to go to the land which He said He would show him. He journeyed in faith and obedience. In verse 8 we read of what happened when he had reached the hills east of Bethel. It was an area between two places; Bethel (which means, as we said earlier, 'house of God' or 'God's presence') and Ai (which represents the world). It was here that he pitched His tent and built an altar to the Lord. Heather saw this as an important picture for us all to learn from, especially in relation to worship. For we need to be in such a place that, as we hear from God in worship, we have something of His very heart and presence to take out into the world. And in that which she received from the Lord she sought avenues of expression to others, because she also wanted them to hear from Him.

Increasingly over the years, much of our life was spent in travelling to many places around the world where we had been invited to minister, as God directed our paths. Therefore, we spent a lot of time in the so called 'public arena'. Drawing aside to hear from God was foundational to Heather as she did not want to get caught up in things which were not part of His assignment for her. She wanted to be a carrier of His presence, His aroma, to others. And I believe that something of that beautiful Heaven-scented aroma which she carried from His courts caused many hearts around the world to soften and turn to Him as she shared with them, not least the 'prodigals' who had wandered away. Many felt the love of Father's heart through that aroma, I believe, and had a fresh longing in their hearts to return home. Praise the Lord!

Life below the water-line

As one who sought to experience the depths of His love, Heather was not one who could live in the shallows of life and experience and, therefore, she desired to venture out into the deep with Him. In one of Heather's many personal journals which she kept she wrote these words "If you want to venture into deep waters with God you must be prepared to pay the price! Not the outward show before people but in the hidden things they do not see. The time spent before God seeking Him; in studying and meditating on His Word; in listening for His voice; and in putting into practice what He says." In a word it is 'intimacy', which the dictionary describes as *very personal, deep-seated, private, secret, close.* In essence, everything that our loving God desires to share with us!"

"Going deeper with God", writes Heather, "means we will have a better 'keel' to go through the deeper waters of life." (The dictionary definition of a 'keel' is *the part of a boat extending along the bottom from stem to stern, adding weight, depth and balance and supporting the whole frame*). She goes on to speak of an article which she read in a newspaper about a cross-Atlantic yachtsman named Michael Plant who, in 1992, planned to sail from the USA to France. He wanted everything to be just right for his journey, so he put vast amounts of money into the fittings and fixtures on board his sailing vessel, and he invested even more in the radar equipment, the best there was, because he considered this to be vitally important. But just two weeks into his crossing he hit a really bad storm off the Azores and he was lost overboard. There had been no SOS call and, as all contact was lost with him, a search was launched. These sailing vessels are designed to take the pounding of the waves and they do not normally capsize, but when the vessel was sighted it was upside down in the water, with the radar still working, but with a broken keel. Because the storm had hit suddenly at night there he had no time to put out the distress signal. He had put his effort and money into things that could be seen but he had not paid enough attention, or spent enough time, building a structure that would hold in a storm."

"Time!" A gift we have all been given *equally*, and we can all choose what we do with that gift (how we spend it) whether we use it or waste it! Time spent getting to know Him more is never wasted! Psalm 139 reminds us very clearly that we have all been created by God and given a 'life-time', however long or short that is. A 'life-time' to choose our own priorities, whether to go our own way, doing what pleases us, or to seek God's way; choosing to draw near to Him where we can enjoy an intimate relationship with Him in whatever situation we are walking through, knowing that He IS God and that He delights in us.

The Bible does not speak about the need to be prepared for the storms of life **if** they come, but **when** they come, for storms are a reality of life, and oft times sudden ones! I have already spoken of some of the 'storms' which Heather and I had to face along life's journey, but probably one of the most devastating times was when she was told the news that she had breast cancer. It was unexpected news, a sudden storm, so to speak, yet in Heather's journal she writes, 'I have peace, deep peace!' Her security was in the fact that she knew the only One who could impart peace, her Saviour, the Lord Jesus Christ! They were in the boat together in the midst of the storm and that fact was enough to bring Heather peace, for she had 'spent' her time in seeking close fellowship with Him, in strengthening her 'keel', her life with Him below the water-line of life.

The Living Bible speaks of this peace in a beautiful way in Isaiah 26: 3: *He will keep in **perfect peace** all those who trust in Him, whose thoughts turn often to the Lord.* In Heather's own recorded words in one of her journals, which are words of personal testimony to that proven-truth through her own journey, she writes: "You can walk through any test or trial in supernatural peace and joy, but it is up to you to guard your heart and keep your focus on God and His Word. For you depend upon God's Words for God's answers to your situation."

Among the treasured hand-written notes which Heather left were the words of a song which became very special to her over the years, and as she listened to its words they were echoed from her own heart too:

Through It All

I've had many tears and sorrows,
I've had questions for tomorrow,
There's been times when I didn't know right from
   wrong.
But in every situation, God gave blessed
   consolation,
That my trials only come to make me strong.

Through it all, yes through it all,
I've learned to trust in Jesus,
I've learned to trust in God;
Through it all, yes through it all,
I've learned to depend upon His Word.

I've been to lots of places,
I've seen a lot of faces,
There've been times I felt so all alone.
But in my lonely hours,
Yes, those precious lonely hours,
Jesus let me know I was His very own.

I thank God for the mountains,
And I thank Him for the valleys,
I thank Him for the storms He's brought me
   through,
For if I'd never had a problem,

I wouldn't know God could solve them,
I'd never know what faith in God could do.

"For if I'd never had a problem, I wouldn't know God could solve them. I'd never know what faith in God could do", were words which Heather, too, constantly reiterated for she proved that the tough times are the real growing times and she allowed the trials she faced to be life-transforming to her. She wrote: 'It is not the size of the mountain but the strength of the 'mountain-mover' that matters!' and her teaching notes are full of 'snippets' of encouragement to her listeners to trust the Lord— recognising at all times **He is still God. He remains Sovereign.**

A few years ago Godfrey Birtell, a worship leader and song-writer, came to our Family Camp at Taunton and led us in our praise and worship to the Lord. This was a very special time and Heather loved his unique style and especially the way he sought to direct our focus to the One who is worthy of our highest praise. One of the songs which he was inspired to write is entitled *Still God* and it is such a declaration of this unchanging fact. It speaks of a variety of things that happen in our lives, in our families, in our nation and in our world; things which are crises without hope to a non-believer, but a glorious reminder of the hope that remains alive to those who have put there trust in God their Heavenly Father.

There are times for all of us when we hit a crisis. When the path we have to walk is rough and tough and the going is hard. At such times it is so easy for us to turn our focus to the circumstances and find ourselves despairing. But, as Heather discovered, the moment we turn to the Lord and fix our gaze on Him that wonderful 'divine exchange' takes place in our hearts and, like looking through the two lenses of binoculars, we become aware of His sovereignty and of His unfailing goodness. The impartation of His faith to endure begins to come alive from deep within us, and with that faith comes the reality of His presence, that deep assurance that He is with us, providing, protecting and empowering, just as He promised. Never will He leave us; never will He forsake us and even our dictionaries confirm that **never** means 'at no time' and 'on no occasion'. And the wonderful fact is He dwells *within* us!

In Heather's young days as a Christian the chorus of a well-known hymn which was often sung was:

> We have an anchor that keeps our soul,
> Steadfast and strong while the billows roll,
> Fastened to the Rock which cannot move,
> Grounded firm and deep in the Saviour's love.

One of the most risky places to be is when everything is plain sailing. When life is going fine and there are no cares; no worries. At such times it is so easy to get 'casual' with God and drift along on the calm seas, not paying attention to the weight we need to build onto our 'keel'. In computer language, 'you only get out what you put in'. And in a very real sense it is the same in our relationship with God. If we idle through life—feeding on the books, TV programmes, worldly ideas, humanistic thoughts and negative words that the world offers us—our lives are likely to capsize in a storm because there will be no weight below the water-line. We need to have a heart after God like Daniel, who opened his window towards Heaven and prayed three times a day. That is where the weight of his 'keel' was built. **How about us?**

Walking closely with the Lord is the only way to become strong, and remain strong. And so it means that we need to deal with the *little foxes* in our lives *that would spoil the vine* (Song of Songs 2:15) and ruin the vineyards where that 'divine romance' with the Lord blossoms. In order to know the reality of dealing with the 'little foxes' in her own life, Heather used to regularly apply questions that she saw in Scripture to her own life. In Genesis 4 we read of Cain and Abel's bad relationship with each other, and God asks Cain the question, in verse 6 'Why are you angry?' Most of us find ourselves getting angry over things at certain times. It is an emotion we all have, but, as the Scriptures say in Ephesians 4:26, it is possible to recognise that we *are* feeling angry but choose not to sin. As we allow the fruit of the Holy Spirit to be developed in us instead we are strengthening our 'keel'.

In 1 Kings 19 we read of the time when Elijah was feeling bad about himself and he fled to the cave at Horeb. Here we read another of God's questions: "What are you doing here?" We too need to let Him ask us that question when we are seeking to run away rather than facing the realities of life, because He wants us to grow, to be mature and to be strong in our life below the water-line, trusting Him through everything that He allows.

Again in John 21: we read those very piercing words of Jesus as he repeatedly asked Simon Peter: "Do you truly love me?" We also need to be asked that question, for all too easily we allow people and things to come between us and God, our spouse, our children, our home, our career, our possessions, even Church or people that God has used in special ways in our lives. However good and meaningful these things are, they can all take God's 'first-love' place in our lives and leave us in a place of weakness rather than strength when the storms hit.

Eyes fixed on the goal

Heather was one who was so aware right from the time she became a child of God that she was a traveller; and her heart was set on pilgrimage and her eyes were fixed on the goal of her eternal home. Even when the route took her through the Valley of Baca, that place of weeping, she purposed to make it *a place of springs* (Psalm 84:6) for she knew she was just 'passing through' it was not her final destination! God enabled her to go from strength to strength as she journeyed, secure in the knowledge that He would be both her sun and shield along the way; that He would bestow His blessings, His favour and honour, and that no good thing would He withhold from her as she trusted Him. These were not just words to Heather, they were promises she believed with all her heart, because she had proved that God says what He means and means what He says!

But it is not just when we are going through the valleys that our attitude can hinder what God wants to reveal to us. Many times we are reluctant to let go of the good things in order to move on to the next phase of our journey. *Good, it is said, is the enemy of the best.* How true this is. When we think of our childhood days, perhaps we easily recall many things that we really enjoyed. They were good; they were fun; and we wanted them last for ever! But in order to grow up we have needed to leave those things behind and move on to the other stages in our growth and maturity. He always has new and fresh things for us to move into as He leads us on along that journey with Him, for His desire is to change us from one degree of glory to another; to grow us up, to transform us into His likeness, and that can't happen if we decide to remain where we are rather than to move on.

Being transformed into 'His likeness' means that there is a need for our characters to be shaped and honed along the way. Being changed from one degree of glory to another means that our appearance will be different too — from the inside out! For He wants us to reflect His glory and to show forth that radiance as 'pure gold' tried in the furnace; gold that just oozes out of the cracks and overspills to cover the defects and chips of our marred 'clay vessels' so that all the glory may go to Him and not to us. Fully aware of what it would cost, Heather did not shrink back from this transformation process, even though she knew it meant His furnace of life would need to become hotter in order to bring that purification and show forth the weight of His glory, for she wanted her life to be as pure gold for Him.

It is often so hard to watch others walking that path, isn't it, especially those near and dear to us. Everything in us wants to say 'stop, that's enough', because our natural human response is to want to shield them from suffering. But if we could, the result would be like taking a pair of scissors and cutting a butterfly free from its cocoon before that fresh new life that was forming was fully developed. Many times I cried tears with her as the furnace got hotter, but Heather never doubted God or the need for more of His refining in her life. Her one desire was to emerge more fashioned into the likeness of her Saviour. And she did, every time and, like me, so many saw those beautiful new aspects of His compassion, grace and power flowing through her life and ministry as a result.

I believe that God allows suffering so that we might be able to have that enlarged capacity to share with others who suffer. Empathy is a God-given quality that He often brings to birth in us through our own sufferings. It enables us to come alongside and in some way enter into others feelings with them in their sorrows, their afflictions, their hurts, their pain, their criticism, their heartaches, their grief, because we have an understanding of what others are facing and walking through. I saw Heather used in this way increasingly as God brought her through times of affliction and she was enabled to not only feel with them with deep compassion, but to encourage them to trust in Him; to lean hard on Him and to draw strength from Him.

Sharing His heart

Heather was a writer not just of books but of precious revelations and responses which she recorded in her journals as she journeyed with Jesus. A prayer she wrote in one of her last journals really touched my heart. It simply reads: "Lord I want Your heart to motivate my life, so that my attitude to anything and everything is pure like Yours." Those words reflect the heart and desire that I saw so clearly in Heather, for she wanted to become more like Jesus in every way.

Philippians 4: 6-7 NIV says: *Do not be anxious about anything, but in everything, by prayer and petition, with thanksgiving, present your requests to God. And the peace of God, which transcends all understanding, will guard your hearts and your minds in Christ Jesus.* As a worshipper, Heather knew that it is impossible to worry **and** worship at the same time, and she was not willing to move out of that place of and adoration. She knew that true worship takes us to the place where we see God on His Throne, and that is all that matters! He was her security at all times and knowing this enabled her to freely worship Him, along the smooth or rough paths of life. So often Heather had taught that 'true worship transforms us into the likeness of the One we worship' and she didn't want to miss any opportunity to seek His face and touch His heart with her love. She had faith in His promises and, therefore, His peace was the conscious awareness she had that she could trust Him totally, whatever her need, knowing that His abundant resources would not fail to be made available to her.

Those who knew Heather will be aware that she loved sheep; those fascinating creatures so often referred to in Jesus' teaching, and which are never far from our view in the fields or hillsides around us, wherever we might live. It is not surprising then that Heather loved Psalm 23 which opens with David's declaration: *The Lord is my Shepherd, I shall not want.* Or, as the Living Bible says, *Because the Lord is my Shepherd I have **everything** I need!* Heather saw that 'want' holds us captive in the biggest prison in the world! It is the most populated and the most aggressive. It is over-crowded and many of its inmates never leave; they never escape, they never get released. They serve a permanent 'life sentence.' All 'prisoners' are in want; desiring something bigger, better, nicer, finer, faster, thinner . . . they just 'want'. Perhaps just one more thing, a new job, a new car, a new house, or whatever, but their 'want' is never satisfied. But like David, Heather could say 'The Lord is MY Shepherd" and she proved that in Him she had everything she needed. Everything that would really satisfy her soul; for she knew that His lavish giving far exceeds anything that this world could ever offer.

He makes me to lie down in green pastures. He leads me beside still waters. (Psalm 23:2) The shepherds of the day had to work hard to provide 'green pastures', for it meant clearing the ground of rocks and harmful weeds and irrigating the soil. With very little water supply, this meant having to create ways to produce pools of water by removing tree stumps and burning scrub growth. David knew all about this from his days as a shepherd and he knew what it took to make that provision in order to have healthy, satisfied sheep.

Sheep are one of the only animals that do not clean themselves and they are the least able of all of God's creatures to take care of themselves. They are defenceless against their predators, with no fangs and no claws. They can't bite or out-run other creatures. They are dirty and don't even enjoy a dip in the river like a dog, or like birds in the pool. When they are dirty, without help they stay that way! Heather would so often remind us of how like sheep we all are 'spiritually' and of how God's metaphor fits us perfectly. We can do nothing for ourselves. We rely totally on our Shepherd for everything.

Even for those who love sheep, it has to be recognised that they are one of the dumbest animals God created. They get themselves in the most stupid (and dangerous) situations and constantly need rescuing, especially when they stray too near the boundaries where predators roam. Sounds familiar! So many times in Scripture God calls us

'His sheep'; *those of His very own pasture*, because He Himself knows just how much we are like them and need His Shepherd care and protection. Its is a delightful scene to watch shepherds at work among their own flocks, and to see how the sheep respond when they hear the voice of their own shepherd calling them closer for expressions of his tender care or to lead them to fresh pastures. How it must bless the heart of our Shepherd when we respond that way too!

To be able to hear the distinct voice of our tender Shepherd above all that would seek to distract us or clamour for our attention is very precious; and to know, too, that He has done everything, through His sacrifice for our sins on the Cross, that provides for us to be able to 'lie down' (rest) in His finished work! In that place of 'wanting nothing',where His supply is complete and total for us to draw on. Where, among the tender, dew-fresh 'green pastures' we are well-nourished and well-watered *beside His quiet waters*. For Jesus, our Shepherd, with His own nail-pierced hands, has made that provision for our souls. He has torn out and destroyed the thorns of condemnation and he has loosed the boulders of sin, replacing them with 'seeds' of His grace and 'pools' of His mercy.

This lovely Psalm reflects so much of what our relationship means with our tender, loving Shepherd, even as the language changes from 'I and He' to 'you and me' as it moves through the verses. Heather loved meditating on all the beautiful analogies that this very personal Psalm contains and many from around the world have testified of the way that the Holy Spirit brought this Psalm alive to them through the teaching and revelation that she shared.

She sought to live in such a way that enabled her to know and enjoy the personal care and provision of her great 'Shepherd' as He nourished, sustained and protected her day by day. And, as we are reminded in the book of Revelation, where John's vision of the Throne in Heaven is recorded, that same Jesus—the Lamb of God at the centre of the Throne, is again spoken of as the 'Shepherd' who leads *the redeemed of the Lord to everlasting springs of living water!* (Revelation 7:17) Praise God, Heather is continuing to know the eternal provision of her Shepherd.

Dwelling in the 'secret place'

Another of Heather's favourite passages was Psalm 91. She delighted in all the promises that were hers, as she learned *to dwell in the secret place of the Most High*, where she knew that she could *remain stable and fixed under the shadow of the Almighty—whose power no foe can withstand.* (Psalm 91:1 AMP) Heather knew that whatever she faced, the Lord would shade and protect her close to His heart in that 'secret place' and so she, too, could echo the words of the Psalmist with confidence: "I will say of the Lord **He is my refuge and my fortress, My God, on Him I lean and in Him I confidently trust.**" How good it is to be able to boast about our Mighty God in this way in the secure knowledge that our lives are hid with Christ in God!

Heather faced many trials and times of testing in her life but she faced them bravely and courageously, believing that what God was allowing her to pass through would enable her to be better equipped for Him. In fact, she would probably be among those who have said that they have learned so much more through those times in the valley, than from life on the mountain top. She knew, and others witnessed to this too, that her life was enriched as she leaned hard on Jesus, the Rock of her Salvation, in that place of close intimacy. This is something which I, too, proved as I walked through times of trials and testing, especially along my own cancer journey. God became so much more real to me and it changed my life (and others would say my ministry, too) through His tender compassion that flowed out to me.

Many little hand-written words of praise and thanks to God were tucked in Heather's journals which bear testimony to this fact. This was one of her favourites.

The Anchor holds

I've journeyed through the long dark night,
Out on the open sea,
By faith alone, sight unknown,
And yet His eyes were watching me!

The anchor holds though the ship is battered,
The anchor holds though the sails are torn,
I have fallen on my knees as I faced the raging
     seas,
The anchor holds in spite of the storm.

I've had visions, I've had dreams,
I've even held them in my hands,
But I never knew they would slip right through
Like, they were only grains of sand.

I have been young, but I'm older now
And there's been beauty these eyes have seen,
But it was in the night—in the storm of my life
That's where God proved His love for me!

Author unknown

Like Paul, who said, *I want to know Christ and the power of His resurrection and the fellowship of sharing in his sufferings . . .* (Philippians 3:10) so Heather desired to accept His invitation to enter into that 'secret place' where communion with Him was the priority for her life. None of us could ever go through the pain and anguish of the sacrifice that Jesus bore for us on the Cross. It is an agony that He bore in our place as the spotless Son of God, once and for all. It is a finished work. But I believe that the *fellowship of His sufferings,* the pain and heartache which He feels for this world as He sees the hungry, the sick, the abandoned, the prisoner, the bewildered, is something we enter into *with Him* when we *go* through experiences of suffering ourselves, in whatever form. When we *come* through what I believe are those God-given times, it's as if we see afresh through His eyes. Our hearing becomes sharper to the cries of those in need, and His compassion is ignited in our innermost beings to respond through the *resurrection power* of His love

Isaiah 61: 1-3 is a wonderful passage and one which Heather went back to often. Why? Because I believe it came alive to her through all that the Lord had allowed her to enter into *with Him*. She knew the humbling reality of those words:

> *The Spirit of the Sovereign* LORD *is on me, because the* LORD *has anointed me to preach Good News to the poor. He has sent me to bind up the broken-hearted, to proclaim freedom for the captives, and release from darkness for the prisoners, to proclaim the year of the* LORD's *favour . . .*

> *. . . to comfort all who mourn, and provide for those who grieve in Zion—to bestow on them a crown of beauty instead of ashes, the oil of gladness instead of mourning, and a garment of praise instead of a spirit of despair. They will be called oaks of righteousness, a planting of the* LORD, *for the display of **his splendour**.*

Way back in 1997 Paul E. Billheimer wrote a book, which was published by Christian Literature Crusade, entitled, *Don't waste your Sorrows*. You know, we can all too easily do just that by focusing on the well-worn question "Why me ?" instead of saying "What do you want to show me, Lord ?" I know Heather was constantly asking Him that, because she didn't want to miss anything He had for her, and I never once heard her say "Why me?" because I don't believe it was ever in her thinking. She couldn't do anything other than reach out to those she found herself among who were experiencing the pain of their *sufferings*, because she knew that the Spirit of the Lord and His anointing was upon her.

Knowing Him

When we are 'born again' and come into that very personal living relationship with Him, we start a journey with Him that unfolds an ever-increasing awareness of His passion and plans for us, through His amazing love which is shed abroad in our hearts. And just as a marriage is strengthened when a husband and wife tell each other how much they love each other and how much they mean to each other, so our faith and relationship with Jesus is enriched as we express the *incomparable greatness* of knowing Him as our Lord and Saviour. Being aware that what we have gained in Christ, that Pearl of great price, makes everything else seem so worthless.

But as Heather knew so well, to really *know* Him and His *incomparable greatness* takes a lifetime of walking together with Him through all the variety of life's paths and situations, the mountains and the valleys. In pressing through the pain barriers when we don't always see our own immediate healing or release, and others do. In trusting Him totally when life doesn't make sense, and there are no answers to our questions.

As we look at the passage in Philippians 3 NIV, which I referred to earlier, we realize that in the earlier verses of that chapter (verses 7 and 8) Paul is really using the helpful imagery of a 'bank' and speaking of his own profit and loss account! *But whatever was to my profit I now consider loss for the sake of Christ. What is more, I consider everything a loss* **compared to the surpassing greatness of knowing Christ Jesus my Lord**, *for whose sake I have lost* [let go of] *all things. I consider them rubbish, that I may gain Christ and be found in him . . .* The Amplified Bible describes that knowledge as *Progressively* *becoming more deeply acquainted with Him; of perceiving and recognizing and understanding Him more fully and clearly.* That takes a life time's walk of devotion and trust. No quick fixes. No short cuts . . . *that I may [actually] be found and known as* **in Him,** *not having any [self-achieved] righteousness that can be called my own . . . but possessing that [genuine righteousness] which comes through faith in Christ (the Anointed One), the [truly] right standing with God, which comes from God by [saving] faith.* (Philippians 3:9 AMP) Those words sum up so clearly just how Heather wanted to be known and why, I believe, He could use her so powerfully.

Those who knew Heather will be aware that she was a 'one hundred per cent' person in her faith and commitment to the Lord, and in everything she sought to do. There were never any 'half measures, and she certainly could not have been described as 'lukewarm'. She was totally Christ-centred and remained 'red hot' in her passion and love for the Lord, and her growing desire right to the end was the same as that expressed by Paul in Philippians 3:12 . . . *I press on to take hold of that for which Christ Jesus took hold of me.* All the joys and blessings of her steps of faith, and life's trials, just made her even more eager to say, "Forgetting what is behind, (the rough paths and the smooth)—"I strain towards what is ahead." Yes, she longed to serve Him in every way she could, but from a heart like Mary; as one who that sat at His feet to love, to learn, to worship so that she would have a growing knowledge and understanding of Him to both enjoy and pass on to others.

Heather's personal journals are full of priceless little 'gems' that God gave her as she journeyed with Him, many of which came as she knew she needed to dig deep in God, and He gave her a jewel 'mined' from the deep places. For me it is like opening up a treasure chest and finding there some precious 'gathered gold'; nuggets of Truth that

Heather found and sought to apply to her life and which strengthened her for her journey with Him (and many others along the way too) right to the end.

As her husband it is a privilege to give a little window into her own very precious and personal walk with the Lord and of the closeness of relationship they enjoyed together. But I guess, knowing Heather, she would have wanted to leave us all with a challenge! *How would you describe your profit and loss bank account?* Probably at this moment in time, in the midst of a credit crisis, many of us would say, "not too healthily right now!" But would you be honest enough to apply this same question to your relationship with the Lord? Do you so value Him *above* everything that your one desire is to *know* more of Him, whatever it costs? Are you making the right use of your time, and His resources, to add strength to the 'keel' of your boat so that, however much the storms and tides of life lash and batter, you are strengthened below the 'water-line' as you seek to nourish your inner being on Him, as Heather did, so that you are well equipped to make your journey home too?

May the choices which she made, amid the challenges which she faced, help you to face those same questions as you ponder on her testimony.

A Tapestry of Testimonies

Our example should be such
that others may safely follow.

C. H. Spurgeon

Some of the things that I really treasure around the home are the wonderful tapestries which Heather made because they constantly remind me of aspects of her life. I often think of the times we shared together as Heather was quietly stitching (*and reading too!*) whilst I was writing or reading. For us it was a time of enjoying the sweet presence of the Lord together as we relaxed together and listened to a worship CD or as we just appreciated each other's company.

I think of the plan Heather had in mind as she held those empty canvasses in her hands before ever a stitch was crafted, and it reminds me of the amazing and awesome fact spoken of in Ephesians 1: 4 of how He chose me (you) *before the foundation of the world* and had a plan for my life— and yours.

Thinking of Heather holding a whole pile of threads to work into the 'masterpiece' she was creating, reminds me of how God created each one of us to be so uniquely special. Psalm 139:13 and 15 (in the Amplified Bible), reads: *For You did form my inward parts; You did knit me together in my mother's womb . . . My frame was not hidden from You when I was being formed in secret [and] intricately and curiously wrought [as if embroidered with various colours].* Stitch by stitch to create each one of us as His own 'masterpieces'! What an awesome fact.

I think, too, of the way she lovingly created each tapestry, and the patience and commitment she had to complete the work she had begun, however long it took. My thoughts go to that lovely promise recorded in Philippians 1: 6 . . . *that he who began a good work in (me) you will carry it on to completion . . .* I am so glad that He never gives up on us but is committed to complete what He has begun, however long it takes!

One thing I was very aware of as Heather was in the process of working on those lovely pictures was that the underside, with all its rougher 'finishing off' threads and sometimes a blurring of colours and patterns, was very different from what was taking shape on the upper side of the canvas. It is a reminder of how important it is to keep our eyes on what God is doing in our lives from His perspective rather than focusing on what isn't taking shape from our perspective, otherwise we see a very different picture. God always has a beautiful 'new creation' in view!

A Tapestry
of Testimonies

Those completed tapestries constantly remind me of the wonder of God's creation in all its beauty, and of the beautiful multi-talented wife He gave me in Heather—whose life's 'tapestry' on this earth has now been completed. It seems fitting, therefore, that the final part of this book should be a weaving together of a variety of selected threads of testimony in thanksgiving to God for her life.

❋

Dear Heather will be remembered for her great encouragement to me many times – but especially when we were on mission together in the Seychelles. She really was a very special person and I thank God that I was privileged to know her.

❋

Thank you for your messages, Heather. I'm so proud of your life.

❋

We had only been married around a year and had just been to our first Camp. I decided to write to Heather, but in the back of my mind I did not think she would reply. A few days later I had a personal letter back from her with the Scripture—"For I know the plans I have for you, says the Lord." I have held on to that Scripture in all the twenty-five years we have been married. Heather certainly practised what she preached!

❋

Memories of a lovely and much loved lady.

❋

❋

Heather understood and practised 'generational transfer'.
Thank you Heather for your example.

❋

Charm is deceptive and beauty does not last, but a woman who
fears the Lord will be greatly praised. (Proverbs 31: 30)

❋

I thank God for Heather's sense of fun. In November 2005 I was
at the Ladies Conference at High Leigh. It was my 50th birthday
and my friend had brought me a huge chocolate cake to celebrate.
Heather thought it right to use this for Communion. It was so
right. Such a sense of love and fun with His girls! I thank God
for her obedience.

❋

Bless you Lord for Heather. It has been a privilege to know her
and be a friend. She blessed our lives—and the lives of our
children. Thank you for your prayers. Forever in our
memories—with love.

Remembered as a woman of God who brought words that lifted
people Heaven-ward.

❋

I thank the Lord for Heather. Even though I did not know her, I
felt I did. I loved her like a close friend because through her
example, love and teaching she influenced my life and those of
my family. Special memories.

❋

Thank you, Heather, for your prayers and love for me. You
always made me feel so special and important—however silly
my need might have seemed. I miss you, but thank God for your
life.

❋

✤

May God continue to bless her books and teaching legacy—as she enjoys His presence!

✤

I always felt that Heather would have hugged the world for Jesus if she could. She was so faithful in all she did. The world is a better place because she was here—and now she is in the best place ever!

✤

We praise God with you for the life of Heather. She was a great encouragement to us. We thank God for the times at Camp. Also for the marriage weekends and our Israel visit with our whole family.

✤

My daughter was 5 weeks old when one day I tripped over on a muddy path with her in my arms. I handed her over to Don and Heather who were behind me. Heather held her and cradled her for as long as was necessary. On more than one occasion during that Camp, Heather held her for me. I was so grateful.

✤

Heather prayed for me when there was a word of knowledge about bad experiences at school. I remember Heather's teaching on 'The Blood of Jesus' in particular. I also remember her teaching on 'names' and the importance of names in Jewish thinking. There was an 'altar call' for people who had been called negative names throughout their lives to receive healing. I also went forward for prayer because of my own name being a pagan one. I give thanks from my heart for Heather's teaching. May I be a baton carrier!

✤

You have left behind a big hole in our hearts, but we know God will fill it up. You have touched the hearts of so many people over the years. May you still be teaching in those Heavenly gates!

✤

Heather's giggle that interspersed her teaching always made me feel greatly loved and incredibly close to her. It also helped to bring the message she was preaching 'home' to me. I shall miss her — and her giggle — loads! She was a wonderful mother in God.

Heather's ministry lives on. It lives on in the lives of those she touched, including ours. I found myself crying gently through most of the service yesterday. Crying, not for her passing so much as for a sense of how grateful I am for her example; for having had a chance to be blessed by her ministry. As a guy I probably saw this through the impact Heather's unswerving faith had on my wife, Linda, through the Ladies Conferences especially. I thank God for all that Heather was, is and will be!

With grateful thanks to God for your life and ministry.

We are so grateful to God for Heather. Her warmth, her very inspiring, nourishing and strengthening teaching — demonstrated in her life. We shall miss her at Camp very much, but still be inspired and encouraged when we remember her and all she stood for. She is cheering us on still in Heaven! Thank you for your 'family' ministry — taught in word and in how you live.

Thank you Heather for all your teaching. I was saved at a GNC mission many years ago. I was impacted by your teaching on fear, anxiety and depression. Our family have been built on your teaching. The Service touched a spot on Monday. I will take with me something which you often said — 'Course you can!' — and hope I will live up to it.

I am still His because of the way Heather helped me.

✤

To God be the glory great things He has done. And one of those was Heather. Her example as a wife, mother, grandmother, teacher, writer . . . and the list goes on was amazing. We thank God for Heather's life and the memory of her.

✤

I thank God for this truly remarkable lady.

✤

What we now know to be her last message at Camp in 2006 spoke particularly into my life. Her serenity when I went to thank her will stay with me always. Although we know the 'baton' is being passed on, I will miss her when I come to Camp.

✤

I will always remember the time Heather prayed for me at one of the earlier Ladies Conferences. She asked the Holy Spirit to bring confidence—a word from the Lord. I praise God for that special time which launched me into a team leading Ladies events in our local area. Certainly one who heard from God.

✤

Thank you for all your love and encouragement. My prayer is that I will be able to have a similar spirit in a small measure!

✤

Heather has touched so many hearts and has inspired many with her teaching. Her teaching on 'The Blood of Jesus' will stay with me always! Although there seems to be something missing from Camp this year, I know God is sovereign and that, of course, is something which Heather helped us to always keep in mind.

✤

Thank You, God, for a lovely godly woman in Heather, who was always ready to pray and be interested in people, and to go where You led her.

✤

❖

Thank you for explaining about the importance of keeping short accounts.

❖

A ruby with endless pearls of wisdom. A warrior of Christ to the end—probably even more. Busy for the Kingdom now!

❖

'Of course you can'! Thank you Heather for all you have done.

❖

Teaching from Heather on the family was so vital for us because we received none such teaching elsewhere. It was a pleasure to hear Heather develop as a teacher and preacher.

❖

It was a joy and a pleasure to know Heather and to sit under her teaching. Over the last few years I saw God's anointing increase as her messages to us grew more and more challenging and directive. We travelled part of our journey along the same route and Heather was always supportive to me. I thank God for her and that He released her to the Body of Christ.

❖

Thank You. I rejoice in God because of you and your faithfulness.

A very down to earth encouraging Bible teacher. Thanks Heather.

I praise God for Heather, who clearly touched thousands of lives, in a very quiet and unassuming way.

A very special sister and friend whose life showed me so much about what it really means to love the Lord Jesus with all your heart, soul, mind and strength.

Many women have done noble things, but you surpass them all.

I owe Heather more than I can explain. We only ever spoke once. I was just a 'camper' at a Ladies Conference! I was upset, angry, confused—and in just a few words, a warm smile and a private conversation, she helped me to put things right. But also my every day freedom to be 'me' I owe to her. For years I was a Martha, who wanted to be a 'Mary' and couldn't. In an address at Camp she said 'loving other people in need is loving God' I was free to be 'me' because I can do that. Bless you and your lovely family.

Several years ago I attended the Ladies Conference at Coventry. One of the visual aids that Heather gave us was some Sweet Pea seeds from her garden, with instructions on how to plant them when we got back home. I followed the instructions carefully and to my surprise and delight I had beautiful Sweet Peas in my garden all summer and now have them every year as a result of a few tiny seeds! The fragrance is so delicate and strong—it reminds me of the fragrance of Jesus.

I was also blessed with one of Heather's gifts. A lovely card with encouraging words, which were exactly right at that particular time. Thank you for your love and passion for Jesus.

I have sat at the feet of Heather over the years as she has taught and shared what God has been teaching her from His Word. There are so many memories of a smiling Heather and her honest 'feet on the ground' approach. I shall always treasure an embroidery I was given at a Ladies Conference with the same text on it which was given to me when I was very young. Thank you for all the love and blessing you have been over the years.

Heather. A truly gifted and strong woman of God who gladly submitted her gifts and her strengths to His will and by so doing became a channel of His blessing to many people.

I shall always remember Heather with great affection. I had not realized that anyone could be so kind and friendly to a stranger. I learned a lot through her attitude to life. If she could enjoy doing anything because God asked her to do it then I could start doing so too! Her attitude to life changed mine. With love and gratitude.

From the hundreds of letters and cards we have received from around the world, these testimonies have, not surprisingly, been repeated time and time again by people of all ages, tribes and tongues. The Lord truly blessed her life—and as He did she was such a channel of His blessing to others.

Finally, through the pages of this book we have already read of tributes brought through a dear friend, Carlyn, who officiated at Heather's Thanksgiving Service. She wrote these words and brought them to Heather while she was so ill in the Hospice as a fitting final testimony and acrostic of her name—

> **H**oly woman of God
> **E**arnestly creative and full of industry
> **A**nointed speaker and leader
> **T**rue and loving wife
> **H**appy homemaker
> **E**vergreen fingers encouraging growth
> **R**adiant with God's glory

And now—all glory to him who alone is God, who saves us through Jesus Christ, our Lord; Yes, splendour and majesty, all power and authority are his from the beginning; his they are and his they evermore shall be. And he is able to keep you from slipping and falling away, and to bring you, sinless and perfect, into his glorious presence with mighty shouts of everlasting joy. Amen!

Jude verses 24 and 25 LB

Dear Reader,

As you have read through this book maybe your heart has been stirred by Heather's life story; the trust she had in God; the firm belief she had in the promises of God as recorded in His Word—The Bible; or the way that she was able to walk with Him day-by-day—even when the path was rough and tough. You may be asking 'how can I know a personal relationship with the Lord Jesus Christ too that will open up a whole 'new life' of walking with Father God—moment by moment?'

Or maybe you are facing some difficult life issues right now which have raised questions you would like to talk with someone about.

We would count it a real privilege to help you to understand the wonderful love that God has for you and the plans and purposes He desires for your life. You may contact me at the following address:

GOOD NEWS CRUSADE,
17 High Cross Street,
St. Austell,
Cornwall.
PL25 4AN

God bless you–
Don Double

HEARING GOD SPEAK
Don Double

The most awesome moments of life have to be hearing God speak. Don Double shares from almost half a century of experience of how God has spoken at significant times in his life. He draws from the Bible, teaching that hearing God speak is totally Scriptural and can be normal for every believer. In *Hearing God Speak* Don reveals eighteen ways that he has heard God speak to him on specific occasions.
Price £5.99

HEALING THE JESUS WAY
Don Double

Even a quick reading of the Gospels reveals that Jesus healed people. He healed them in a variety of ways. He healed those who came to Him. Whoever you are, whatever your condition know that Jesus can heal you. *Healing the Jesus Way* contains up to date testimonies of God's healing power that will encourage your faith and point you to the Healer—Jesus.
Price £5.99

BREAKTHROUGH INTO FREEDOM
Don Double
Conquering depression, anxiety, fear and worry

Most people have, at some point in their life, faced these problems. Jesus Christ promised abundant life for all those who love Him. This book teaches clearly how you can enjoy the fullness that is available through Jesus Christ's provision.

Price £3.50

BE REAL ABOUT GUIDANCE
Don Double

Every Christian needs two types of guidance— everyday leading and guidance for big decisions. People need help concerning life-changing issues. It is important to get this right. This book teaches about the principles that help you to make those right decisions.

Price £5.99

LOVE IS SPELT T.I.M.E.
Don and Heather Double

How much time do we give to the people we love? The title of this extremely practical book based on 1 Corinthians 13, came from a conversation between a father and his teenage daughter. This remark reminds us all that we need to use the time we have to express love to those closest to us. Read this book and learn for yourself why Love is spelt T.I.M.E.

Price £3.50

OUCH! THAT HURT
Heather Double

Whoever we are we all experience things in life that hurt us and subsequently live under these hurts. Some of these hurts come through close family relationships. This book looks at how some characters in the Bible were hurt and what happened because of those hurts. It will take you to the Cross of Jesus Christ and see how we can be freed from all such hurts.

Price £5.99

HEAVEN'S BLUEPRINT
FOR MARRIAGES BUILT ON EARTH
Don and Heather Double

"Heaven's Blueprint" seeks to teach in an uncompromising way God's concepts for marriage found in the Scriptures. The message comes through clear that the covenant relationship of marriage is still the best and most enjoyable for any couple and gives stability in facing life's challenges.
Price £9.99

FIVE FACTS OF LIFE
Don Double

Now translated into many different languages, ten of thousands from around the world have been helped through this booklet.
Price 60p